RATIONAL-EMOTIVE THERAPY WITH ALCOHOLICS AND SUBSTANCE ABUSERS

D0023791

Titles of Related Interest

Agras EATING DISORDERS:
Management of Obesity, Bulimia and Anorexia Nervosa
Kirschenbaum TREATING CHILDHOOD AND
ADOLESCENT OBESITY
Knott ALCOHOL PROBLEMS
Miller THE ADDICTIVE BEHAVIORS
Rhodes/Jason PREVENTING SUBSTANCE ABUSE
AMONG CHILDREN AND ADOLESCENTS
Weiss TREATING BULIMIA: A Psychoeducational Approach

Related Journals

ADDICTIVE BEHAVIORS
ALCOHOL AND ALCOHOLISM
ALCOHOL AND DRUG RESEARCH
CLINICAL PSYCHOLOGY REVIEW
JOURNAL OF SUBSTANCE ABUSE TREATMENT

PSYCHOLOGY PRACTITIONER GUIDEBOOKS

EDITORS

Arnold P. Goldstein, Syracuse University
Leonard Krasner, Stanford University & SUNY at Stony Brook
Sol L. Garfield, Washington University in St. Louis

RATIONAL-EMOTIVE THERAPY WITH ALCOHOLICS AND SUBSTANCE ABUSERS

ALBERT ELLIS
JOHN F. McINERNEY
RAYMOND DiGIUSEPPE
RAYMOND J. YEAGER
Institute for Rational-Emotive Therapy

Allyn and Bacon
Boston • London • Toronto • Sydney • Tokyo • Singapore

ISBN 0-205-14434-9

Printed in the United States of America

11 10 9 8 7 6 5   04 03 02 01 00 99

Library of Congress Cataloging in Publication Data

Rational emotive therapy with alcoholics and substance
abusers.
(Psychology practitioner guidebooks)
Bibliography: p.
Includes index.
1. Substance abuse—Treatment. 2. Alcoholism—
Treatment. 3. Rational emotive psychotherapy. I. Ellis,
Albert. II. Series. [DNLM: 1. Alcoholism—therapy.
2. Psychotherapy. 3. Substance Abuse—therapy.
WM 420 R2368]
RC564.R38 1988   616.86'1   87–22080

To Janet, Barbara, Dorothy and Carolyn

Acknowledgment

The authors would like to extend a special thanks to Dorothy Sharlip-DiGiuseppe for reading an early draft of this manuscript and providing editorial comments and corrections.

Contents

Chapter 1
Introduction

Originated by Albert Ellis in 1955, Rational-Emotive Therapy has become one of the most comprehensive, integrative, and popular schools of psychotherapy ever practiced (Bernard & DiGiuseppe, in press; Corey, 1985, 1986; Gutsch, Sisemore, & Williams, 1984; Heesacker, Heppner & Rogers, 1982; Smith, 1982; Weinrach, 1980). Ellis, as a psychoanalyst, had already found that although his clients were benefitting from their therapy, their gains were not attributable to their reliving of past events, bringing unconscious motivations into consciousness, getting "in touch" with their feelings, or by "working through" the transference relationship. Rather, clients' disturbed feelings and behaviors largely changed because of their newly acquired thinking.

Besides becoming disenchanted with the existing therapeutic theories, Ellis found that he could help clients overcome their disturbances through more direct, time- and cost-efficient means. Rather than passively listening to their free associations, Ellis began helping clients actively challenge and dispute their dysfunctional, irrational, and antiempirical beliefs and to act against them. Thus, Rational-Emotive Therapy (RET) became a cognitively and behaviorally oriented theory and practice, emphasizing active, directive, and systematic interventions in the here-and-now (Ellis, 1957a, 1957b, 1958a, 1962).

RATIONAL-EMOTIVE THEORY

Rational-Emotive Therapy differs from other major schools of psychotherapy in the importance it places on the role of cognition in human disturbance. Whereas other therapists primarily focus on past events, unconscious processes, and environmental contingencies, RET concentrates on people's *current* beliefs, attitudes and self-statements as contributing to or "causing" and maintaining their emotional and

1

behavioral disturbances. RET does not overlook biological, genetic, cultural or environmental factors as influences on human functioning, but emphasizes humans' innate capacities to change their thinking in order to live happy and productive lives (Ellis, 1962, 1971, 1973a, 1985a; Ellis & Becker, 1982; Ellis & Bernard, 1983, 1985; Ellis & Grieger, 1977, 1986; Ellis & Harper, 1975).

THE ABCs OF HUMAN EMOTION

In the course of their daily lives, people are commonly faced with numerous stressors as well as difficult and challenging life events. Some common negative life events include: the break-up of a marriage, the loss of a job, rejection, time pressures at work, unemployment, the death of a loved one, failure at a task, and the like. Often associated with these unpleasant events are intense, negative, inappropriate, emotional reactions, such as depression, anger, frustration, guilt, anxiety, and embarrassment. Although negative life events are likely to be accompanied by negative emotional states, these events *do not directly cause our emotional reactions.*

If life's unpleasantries and stressors do not cause or *activate* disturbed emotional reactions, where do they come from? This question is best answered by considering the ABCs of Rational-Emotive Therapy.

According to the ABC Model of RET, negative life events we often confront are called *Activating Events,* or *As,* and the emotions and behaviors that subsequently accompany these events are called the *Consequences,* or *Cs.* Whereas people *traditionally* argue that negative Activating Events in their lives (or in their pasts) actually *cause* their current distress, RET holds that it is their *thoughts* and *beliefs* or *Bs,* about Activating Events that primarily and more directly cause their disturbances (Bard, 1980; Dryden, 1984; Ellis, 1985a, 1985b; Grieger & Boyd, 1980; Grieger & Grieger, 1982; Walen, DiGiuseppe & Wessler, 1980; Wessler & Wessler, 1980).

A = Activating event
B = Beliefs, attitudes, thoughts, self-statements
C = Emotional and behavioral Consequences

TESTING THE ASSUMPTION
THAT A CAUSES C

Let us test the traditional assumption that the activating events in clients' lives directly cause their feelings. To do so, we will submit the hypothesis that A → C to the following tests.

Test 1. If it is a law of the universe that a particular activating event causes a particular emotion, then it would have to cause that emotion in *everyone*. However, as we all know, different people are likely to feel different things even under identical situations. How, then, do we account for the fact that different people can have different emotional consequences, Cs, to the same Activating Event A? Answer: Because different people can and do think differently about the same Activating Event. Since their emotions stem mainly from their thoughts and beliefs rather than from the event itself, people can feel differently in response to the same event.

Suppose, for example, that we survey 100 parents of drug and alcohol-abusing children. The important *Activating Event* for these parents would be the same. A is that their child has a substance-abuse problem. Despite being faced with the *same* activating situation, we can predict many different emotional consequences.

A (Activating Event) = child abuses controlled substance
C1 (Consequence) = anger
C2 (Consequence) = depression
C3 (Consequence) = acceptance

The emotion experienced, whether it is anger, depression, or acceptance, depends not on the event itself, but rather on what each particular parent thinks or believes, B, about their child's having a substance abuse problem. A, therefore, contributes to, but does not cause C; rather, more directly, B causes C.

If the parents think, at B, that they are total failures as parents and that it is awful and tragic that their child is addicted, then they are likely to *get themselves* depressed. However, if they think of the addiction as something to work hard at overcoming and as an obstacle in their child's life path, then they will be more accepting of their child and more geared toward taking positive steps to help their child. The emotion experienced, C, mainly follows, therefore from their beliefs, B, about their child's problem A.

Test 2. The connection between thoughts and feelings is also clarified by tracing the emotions of just one individual. Consider the previous example where a parent has a child who has a drug or alcohol problem. If the *fact* that their child has a problem *causes* their anger, for example, how do we account for the times when the parent feels less angry about it or even feels accepting and motivated to be supportive and to help out? The changes in the parents' emotions, Cs, are clearly a function of the changes in what they say to themselves at B about their child's problem, A.

Table 1.1.
A (Activating Event) = drug = abusing child

B1 (Belief) it is catastrophic	B2 (Belief) it is an obstacle
C1 (Consequence) depression, frustration	C2 (Consequence) concern, acceptance

If a child's drug problem (the *A*) directly causes a parent's distress, *C*, then the parent would have no recourse but to feel distressed always. That would mean that as long as the child has the problem, the parent must be distressed. Of course, we know that over time parents do *change the way they think about* their children's problems. They decatastrophize them and accept the fact that their child might always have the problem. Here, even though the Activating Event does not change, by changing their thinking about it, parents change their emotions.

Even if the child is rehabilitated, it does not change the fact that a drug problem once existed. If having a child with a drug or alcohol problem directly causes depression, even rehabilitation would not change the past Activating Event and the parents would forever have to be distressed. We know real cases where parents continue to feel embarrassed about their children's pasts as well as cases where they come to accept the past for what it was. The way parents feel, in this example, depends upon how they consciously or unconsciously *decide* to look at their children's problems.

Emotions. As stated earlier, emotions are our feelings. They are visceral or bodily events or actions and are generally preceded by cognitions.

Emotions are either positive or negative. Those that are pleasurable to feel, such as happiness and euphoria, are considered to be positive, whereas those that feel unpleasant, such as depression, anxiety, and anger, are negative. RET seeks to maximize positive emotions while minimizing negative ones, particularly disturbed or self-defeating negative feelings. As has been stated previously, the philosophy of RET is hedonistic, and it aims to maximize long-term pleasure while minimizing needless pain.

Although the goal of RET is frankly hedonistic, RET seeks to help clients feel appropriate levels of emotion, *even when they are negative.* It doesn't oppose feelings — but only self-sabotaging feelings. Rather than have clients feel depressed when a bad event occurs, RET teaches them to think more rationally, thereby encouraging a more appropriate feeling of sadness. Although the client is not expected to feel happy or indifferent about being confronted with some negative Activating Event, the goal is to feel appropriate (and often strong) emotion. RET, therefore, doesn't aim to help clients *not to feel*, but rather to help them feel more appropriate.

Continua. Emotions are considered to fall along two separate continua (Continuum A and Continuum B). Extremes of particular emotions go beyond the boundaries of the continuum onto a separate plane. For example, consider the following diagram.

> *Continuum No. 1A*
> No annoyance . . . Slight
annoyance . . . Moderate annoyance . . . Intense annoyance.
> *Continuum No. 1B*
> No anger . . . Slight anger . . . Moderate
anger . . . Intense anger.
> *Continuum No. 2A*
> No concern . . . Slight concern . . . Moderate
concern . . . Intense concern.
> *Continuum No. 2B*
> No anxiety . . . Slight anxiety . . . Moderate
anxiety . . . Intense anxiety.

According to RET, people commonly make a "magical" jump from the first to the second continuum of emotions (from 1A to 1B or from 2A to 2B) by demanding that unpleasant Activating Events *must not* exist and that it is terrible when they do. It would not be appropriate or realistic to help clients to be happy or totally unconcerned when negative events occur in their lives. But it is in their best interest to *not* feel overconcern or anxiety, especially intense anxiety or panic. Helping clients feel annoyed rather than angry; sad rather than depressed; concerned or vigilant rather than anxious or hypervigilant; and regretful rather than guilty helps them a) to feel less disruptive emotions and b) to perform better. Appropriate levels of emotions are less painful to experience, tend to interfere less with one's ability to perform, tend to alienate others less, and help to motivate clients to work to make changes (Ellis, 1985a, 1985b, 1986). The function of emotions will be discussed next.

FUNCTIONAL ANALYSIS

A functional analysis involves helping clients see that their negative emotions are not serving their best long-term interests. It is designed to help them commit to working on changing the ways they feel. For example, angry clients are not usually likely to be motivated to change their anger, partly because they momentarily feel good about putting down others. They want the events in their lives to change. A functional dispute serves to point out to clients that their anger is preventing them from efficient functioning.

Functional disputing can be done by showing clients that their inappropriate emotion usually doesn't feel good and, even when it does, it brings them less pleasure than pain. When they admit this, they will often work to change their dysfunctional feelings.

Clients will also work to change their emotion if they are helped to see that it stands in the way of achieving their goals. This is actually not that difficult for the RET therapist, because numerous examples can be used to show how inappropriate emotions negatively effect clients' performances and tend to alienate others. The Yerkes-Dodson Law illustrates this quite clearly. This law states that as level of arousal (or C) increases, so too does level of performance *to a point* where further increase in arousal becomes detrimental to performance. Think of test taking as an example. If you are too low-keyed or unaroused, you will not likely demonstrate your knowledge on the test. So, too, if you are *over*aroused, you are too tense to do well. The goal, therefore, is to bring your level of arousal down to a manageable and moderate level. That level may be to one of concern rather than anxiety. You can manage this emotional shift by changing what you are telling yourself at B about the pending test. Functional disputing helps clients understand the self-defeating nature of their emotional reactions. This serves to get a commitment from clients to work on changing the way *they* themselves feel. The goal is to feel an appropriate emotion (such as disappointment and sadness at failing) even if it is a negative feeling.

BELIEFS

Beliefs can be, for example, cognitions, thoughts, attitudes, self-statements, or images, and are the primary determinants of emotions. Inappropriate emotions are usually preceded by *irrational beliefs*, whereas appropriate emotions are preceded by *rational beliefs*.

Beliefs are not facts; they are hypotheses. Unlike facts, which are based on observables, hypotheses are testable and challengeable. Thoughts, as hypotheses, are subject to the scientific method of hypothesis testing to determine whether there is empirical evidence to support them. In RET, thoughts and beliefs that lead to self-helping feelings and behaviors, and which usually can be substantiated with empirical evidence and support, are considered to be rational. These beliefs express desires, hopes, and preferences, and are conditional rather than absolutistic. They are based on reality and are verifiable. Irrational beliefs, in RET, are absolutistic and have no empirical evidence to support them or are contradicted by existing data. The following diagram illustrates some differences between rational and irrational beliefs.

Rational	Irrational
1. provable and verifiable	no evidence to support the belief or evidence contradicts the belief
2. associated with appropriate emotions	associated with inappropriate emotions
3. associated with more productive and self-helping behaviors	associated with less productive and self-helping behaviors
4. usually logical and consistent	often illogical and inconsistent
5. usually leads to desirable or happy feelings.	often leads to undesirable or miserable feelings.

CATEGORIES OF IRRATIONAL BELIEFS

Irrational beliefs have several overlapping ingredients. They include: a) demandingness, b) awfulizing c) low tolerance for frustration d) rating of self and/or others, and e) overgeneralizing the future. According to RET Theory, the first irrational belief, grandiose musts and demandingness, tends to lead to the other four (Ellis, 1985a, 1985b; Ellis & Dryden, 1987).

Demandingness. The first category of irrational beliefs are absolutistic demand statements. They come in the following forms: should, must, ought to, have to, need, require, and command. Demands are unyielding, rigid and absolutistic requirements that allow no room for or acceptance of human fallibility. People make irrational demands on themselves, others, the world, the future, and on numerous Activating Events. In doing so, they are, in essence, dictating the workings of the universe.

The RET therapist helps clients see that their demandingness is unfounded, counterproductive, and irrational. Clients are taught to stay with desire and not command that things be different. Wants and preferences are rational and self-helping and lead people to behave in a goal-directed manner.

Awfulizing. When clients evaluate events as *awful*, they magnify or exaggerate the badness of the event. Awful implies that the event could not be any worse than it is, which of course it could be. Things could always be worse. *Awful* also means *more than bad* — which, of course, nothing could be. Clients are taught to appraise things rationally and realistically as bad or as very bad. Considering that which is only bad as something that is awful leads to unnecessary and inappropriate distress. If people accept the fact that bad things *should be* just as bad as they are (right now) because that's the way they indubitably are, they would usually stop their irrational awfulizing.

Low Frustration Tolerance. One of the most significant contributions of RET is its emphasis on low frustration tolerance (LFT), or discomfort anxiety and depression. People tend to believe that they *can't stand* discomfort or frustration. This is nonconsciously thought of as a) "I will die of this hardship!"—which, probably, they won't; or b) "I can't stand this frustration and be happy *at all!*"—which is obviously false. Of course they can, in fact, stand discomfort. It may be hard or even very hard, but is it really ever *too hard* to handle? Evaluating things as *too hard* to handle implies that it is impossible to handle them—which is downright unrealistic and not provable.

Rating of self and others. Madison Avenue often says that you are a better person if you wear designer jeans. Is that true? A scholar might say that smarter people are better people. Is that true? Athletes might say that you are a better person if you are athletically inclined or sports-minded. Is that true? A corporate executive might conclude that you are a better person if you are achievement oriented. Is that true? For that matter, is it true that your human worth is a function of your accomplishments, skills, traits, or values? *Of course not!*

Stopping from rating one's *self* or one's totality is probably the most difficult thing for clients to comprehend and do. They can, however, learn that their worth as a person is *not* contingent upon a rating of their behaviors. When people learn to separate self-worth from rating their behaviors, deeds, and accomplishments, then they are self-accepting. If your worth as a human were contingent upon your performances, your human value would go up and down with each success and failure, which is a most ludicrous notion — and a debilitating notion. But when you insist that you absolutely *must* perform well, you'll frequently make yourself feel worthless when you do a little less well than you supposedly *must* do.

Overgeneralizing about the future. When people insist and command that they *have to* perform well and *must* be approved by significant others, and when they do not fulfill their perfectionist demands, they frequently conclude, "I'll *always* fail hereafter! I'll *never* be able to win approval and be a lovable person!" Then they *really* make themselves anxious and depressed.

SOLUTIONS TO PROBLEMS

Client problems can be addressed two ways. The first is to offer a practical solution and the second is to help clients overcome their emotional obstacles to happiness and goal achievement.

Practical solutions. Practical solutions seek to help clients change the activating events in their lives. This can be done by teaching them specific skills and strategies, such as social problem solving, contingency management, decision making, and communication skills. With newly developed skills, clients can attempt to change their life situations (Ellis, 1971, 1973a, b, c, 1985a; Ellis & Dryden, 1987; Grieger & Boyd, 1980; Walen, DiGiuseppe & Wessler, 1980).

There are two particular problems associated with attempting to change clients' Activating Events. First, the A may not be changeable, and second, the clients' emotions may interfere with their ability to employ the newly learned skills designed to change their A. Their disturbed emotions may, therefore, prevent them from effectively implementing what was learned. Emotional, as well as practical solutions, therefore, had better be sought.

Emotional solutions. Assume, for example, that as a result of training, clients have learned *how* to interact with others at a party. They may have learned what to say, how to say it, and when to listen. For these behaviours to be performed effectively, however, clients had better be at least moderately in control of their emotions. How will they be received if they say the "right things" very anxiously or embarrassedly? Often, too, clients make themselves depressed and don't even try to talk to others at a party. They think to themselves: "Why bother, they won't like me. And if they don't like me, that would prove that I am unlikable and worthless. I would not be able to stand that."

Even if a skill is well learned, clients may feel some degree of anxiety prior to approaching a stranger at a party. If they believe that they can't stand *any* anxiety, their first signs of *appropriate* anxiety may stop them from approaching anyone. It is obvious that unless clients dispute their irrational beliefs and gain greater control over their disturbed emotions, their skill training is likely to go for naught.

Let us go one step further. Suppose that clients do, in fact, approach members of the other sex at a party. Let us also assume that the skills they learned are actually learned quite well. But what if, for any reason, they still are rejected by almost everyone at the party. What if they are unsuccessful at changing the A? Unless they change how they think about being rejected, they are likely to feel very anxious or depressed.

The RET emotional solution, therefore, prioritizes helping clients develop more rational attitudes so that their disturbed feelings won't interfere with their abilities to apply the skills they have learned and so that they won't get themselves inappropriately distressed if they are not successful at implementing these skills (Ellis, 1962, 1973a, b, c, 1985a; Ellis & Dryden, 1987).

STRATEGIES OF THE EMOTIONAL
SOLUTION

As just stated, the emotional solution involves helping clients change their thinking about life events so as to increase the probability of changing A and preventing inappropriate upset when that A proves unchangeable. This philosophy is reflected in what is known as the *Serenity Prayer*:

> Grant me the serenity to accept the things I cannot change
> the ability to change the things I can change
> and the wisdom to know the difference.

Although one often cannot know in advance whether an Activating Event is changeable or not, by opting for the emotional solution and disputing one's irrational beliefs, one will be better able to change them and to be more resilient when they presently can't be changed.

Chapter 2
The Problem with Alcohol

Today, alcoholism is seen as the world's number one public health problem (Alcoholics Anonymous, 1985). Although definitions of alcoholism and alcohol abuse vary somewhat, conservative estimates agree that alcoholics constitute at least 4%, of the general population (Royce, 1981). It is estimated that over 100 million Americans drink alcoholic beverages, between 6 and 10 million adults can be classified as having problems with alcohol use and another million under the age of 21 should be added to this total (Brandsma, 1980). There is considerable variability in subcultural and ethnic patterns of alcohol use and abuse, but it appears that for those who drink, the incidence of alcoholism may well be 8% to 10% (Royce, 1981). When one considers that each alcohol-troubled individual adversely affects the lives of a number of additional others, it has been estimated that as many as 70 million Americans may be suffering from significant personal and social problems attributable to alcohol abuse (Franks, 1985). Further, it is estimated that the economic costs of alcohol and other drug abuse in terms of health care, employee absenteeism, and lost productivity may well amount to an estimated 70 billion dollars annually (Quayle, 1983). Clearly, the personal, social, and economic costs of alcohol problems are staggering.

In recent years there has been a trend toward a broader recognition of alcohol-related difficulties. There appears to be a growing awareness of problems with alcohol and a greater likelihood that severe difficulties with alcohol will be identified by health care professionals, families, employers, and alcoholics themselves. Affected individuals are now more likely to go for help than in the past. Despite considerable controversy about the exact causes of alcoholism and its most effective treatment, there appears to be a trend toward earlier and more direct opportunities for intervention by clinicians.

DEFINITIONS AND DICHOTOMIES

The available literature on the definition, diagnosis, and treatment of alcoholism and substance-abuse problems is truly voluminous. Space does not permit an exhaustive review of this literature nor all of the controversies apparent in it. In some of the literature in the Alcoholics Anonymous tradition (e.g., Alcoholics Anonymous, 1985; Kurtz, 1979) the alcoholic is often referred to as an "all-or-nothing person." Interestingly, much of the controversy in the alcoholism literature also appears to suffer from an all-or-nothing approach.

Rational-emotive theory and therapy has long maintained that all-or-nothing thinking is at the core of much human disturbance (Ellis, 1962), and has advocated correct scientific thinking as a means of achieving psychological adjustment. Consistent with the epistemology advocated by RET, we will attempt to avoid the dichotomous, rigid thinking that permeates the field of substance abuse. Obviously, it would be most difficult to help a group of clients who are predisposed to dichotomous thinking by teaching and modelling dichotomous thinking about their disorder. Consequently, we will employ flexible concepts in formulating treatment and teach flexible thinking to clients.

Traditionalists in treating alcoholism will occasionally be heard saying that being "a little bit alcoholic is like being a little bit pregnant". Despite this attitude, there is an emerging position among researchers that alcoholism is best viewed as a continuum defined by the frequency, amplitude, and duration of problems associated with alcohol and its misuse (Vaillant, 1983). Useful working definitions of alcoholism, therefore, had best avoid creating dichotomous categories instead of a continuous variable. The traditional approach seems to encourage dichotomous and absolutistic reasoning about alcoholism and can therefore be self-defeating.

The *Diagnostic and Statistical Manual DSM III* (American Psychiatric Association, 1980) attempted to integrate some of this recent thinking regarding alcoholism into its diagnostic definitions. Both alcohol abuse and dependence are defined to some extent in terms of the problems attendant upon misusing alcohol. Alcohol abuse is described as repeated use of alcohol despite mounting practical problems. Dependence is seen as alcohol addiction, which results in a definable withdrawal syndrome after stopping or reducing consumption. The implication of these diagnostic categories is that alcohol abuse develops over time, often resulting in varying amounts of physical and psychological dependence.

In Vaillant's (1980, 1983) longitudinal studies of the development of alcoholism in adult males who were repeatedly evaluated over the course of four decades, multiple criteria for alcoholism were employed that focused on the frequency of various operationally defined alcohol-related problems. This study shows the value of using formal or informal adaptation of Vaillant's Problem Drinking Scale (PDS) (Vaillant, 1983). Suspected alcoholics can be questioned regarding the frequency of drinking problems, such as job losses, family complaints, marital problems attributed to drinking, complaints by employers, medical difficulties, blackouts, and absenteeism. The more frequently these difficulties have occurred, the more severe and persistent the drinking problem is likely to be. This approach avoids some of the dichotomous reasoning involved in seeking alcoholism in an all-or-nothing fashion and can lead to authoritative advice to individuals who are experiencing difficulties about effective treatment. When many problems with alcohol are observed over time, the need for effective intervention is established.

The problem-focused approach to alcoholism is particularly consistent with rational-emotive therapy. RET advocates that therapists work to discover clients' emotional, behavioral and social problems (Cs) and work to change them by changing the thoughts, feelings, and actions from which they result. While most alcoholics wish to continue to drink, they do not want the aversive consequences and problems attendant upon their drinking. RET therapists can quickly identify these problems and relate them to a pattern of alcohol abuse, which has often existed for a number of years. They can then see possible changes and ways to work for these changes efficiently and effectively.

DISEASE OR BEHAVIOR DISORDER

Historically, no area involving the study of alcoholism is more fraught with controversy than that regarding its cause. In earlier times, alcohol abuse and dependence was viewed as a moral problem. Alcoholics supposedly lack the will power to regulate their drinking. The problems symptomatic of alcoholism were considered as proof of the immoral nature of the alcoholic.

During the earlier part of this century, alcoholism as a medical and psychological problem began to receive more attention. A hypothetical "allergy" or unspecified disease process that led to an obsession with alcohol and a compulsion to drink was proposed as the cause of the disorder. This concept helped the development of Alcoholics Anonymous (Kurtz, 1979) and defined alcoholism as a medical problem. During the past 50 years, there has also been a trend away from socially stigmatizing admitted alcoholics who seek treatment. Although the

medical model was clearly a step forward, much of the current controversy can be traced to it.

In the earlier Alcoholics Anonymous literature, alcoholism was
thought to be "like a disease". This view stemmed from its often
insidiously progressive course as well as from the frequent failure of
will power alone to insure successful treatment. Today, much of the
metaphorical meaning of this original formulation has been lost and
more *literal* interpretations predominate (Jellinek, 1960). It is probably
equally as inaccurate to view alcoholics as the helpless victims of an
insidious disease as it is to view them as the unenlightened and
sometimes uncooperative sufferers of deficits in moral character.

Vaillant (1983) holds that to understand and study alcoholism, it is
probably best to employ the multifactorial behavioral health or behavioral disorder model. Behavioral or social learning theory researchers
and practitioners (W. R. Miller, 1983, 1985; Marlatt & Gordon, 1985;
Vogler & Bartz, 1982) argue that a strict interpretation of the disease
model may impede treatment of some early stage alcoholics because
they do not view themselves as "diseased" and do not choose abstinence as a goal of treatment. The view one takes of this controversy
depends to some extent on one's vested interest in certain forms of
treatment and also on which end of the continuum of alcoholism one
treats. Seen over its full course, alcoholism appears to be both a
behavioral health disorder and, ultimately for some, a "disease" over
which the individual can exert little control without vigorous treatment
and major life-style changes.

Vaillant (1983) also points out that alcoholism may be considered to
be a disease in the same fashion that medicine refers to essential
hypertension as a disease. Essential hypertension or coronary heart
disease may be defined along a continuum. Its early detection and
treatment requires changes in life-style and the development of more
healthful habits of thought, feeling, and action—rather than medical
intervention alone. As it progresses, however, more and more specific
forms of medical intervention are required. As with alcoholism, effective intervention requires changes in habits of living as well as specific
medical treatment. To consider alcoholism or essential hypertension as
only a physical disease or *only* a product of bad habits may lead to
incomplete and subsequently ineffective treatment at different points
in each disorder. In both cases, individuals with the disease or disorder
are "powerless" over it, as long as their problem is unacknowledged.
Some "power" over the problem is attained by accepting that they have
a disease or disorder and working persistently to change it. Clearly,
then, both conceptions can make important contributions to effective
management and treatment.

CONTROLLED DRINKING VERSUS ABSTINENCE

Nowhere are the differences between a medical and a social learning or behavioral model of alcoholism more controversial than with respect of what is often called the "controlled drinking controversy" (Marlatt, 1983; W. R. Miller, 1983, 1985). This controversy appears to be fueled to a great extent by all-or-nothing thinking on both sides, but consideration of it is appropriate because a client's choice of treatment goals may hinge upon the therapist's views regarding this issue.

Studies of the natural history or course of alcoholism, such as those reviewed by Vaillant (1983), indicate that when individuals are followed throughout their life span some "alcoholics" spontaneously remit or return to "asymptomatic drinking". In their extensive review of treatment outcome literature, Miller and Hester (1980) found an average spontaneous remission or return to asymptomatic drinking rate of approximately 19%. Because some problem drinkers do later control their alcohol use, it was suggested that teaching controlled drinking to alcoholics might yield effective treatment outcomes. As outlined in the reviews noted above, this is quite a controversial issue.

If alcoholism is inevitably progressive, with a deteriorating course in *all* cases, then controlled drinking and self-control treatment strategies are not only ineffective, but dangerous and unethical. A recent review of the use of self-control strategies in the treatment of alcohol abuse by Carey and Maisto (1985) underscored the need for future research. They suggested that self-control treatments have *potential* for *early* intervention in alcohol-related problems; but they concluded that the overall effectiveness of self-control techniques *remains* to be conclusively demonstrated. Available evidence indicates that not all problem drinkers become alcohol dependent, and conversely, that all alcohol-dependent individuals do appear to go through a period of problem drinking. We believe therefore, that self-control strategies or controlled-drinking techniques would be appropriate with individuals who a) are not highly physically dependent on alcohol, b) do not have a long history of frequent alcohol-related problems, and c) are attitudinally flexible enough to work hard at reasserting some degree of control over their alcohol use. Other issues will also influence the clinician's decision to use self-control strategies such as environmental support, social stability, and the individual's view of alcoholism as a disease or behavior disorder. Individualized treatment goals and intervention strategies are therefore suggested. Helping individuals suffering from alcohol problems to learn to acquire a conditional degree of self-control—whether that is achieved through the choice of abstinence, carefully controlled drinking or a combination of both—may be appropriate under various conditions with different individuals. Once an individual has begun to experience long-term, alcohol-related problems and yet continues to consume alcohol dangerously (e.g., five or more drinks at a sitting), however, a progressive-disease behavioral-health disorder exists, which is likely to have far-reaching and potentially life-threatening consequences. Radical change is required to avoid these consequences. A return to take-it-or-leave-it social drinking for such individuals is most unlikely. For any given individual, one can ask: Are the risks of continuing to drink, even in a rigidly controlled fashion, worth it? That, of course, is a question that can only be answered by the individual in treatment, while receiving the best direction available from her or his well-informed therapist.

ETIOLOGY

Despite considerable effort, no support for a single cause for the phenomenon of alcoholism has emerged from nearly 50 years of research. No single biological, psychological, or social cause has been isolated. Although there is encouraging research regarding biological factors, which may further early identification and prevention efforts (Franks, 1985), exact determination of a specific physiological etiology in an individual case of alcoholism is not practical at present. Several in-depth reviews of etiological factors in alcoholism point toward a variety of determinants. These factors include genetic predisposition, cultural and familial patterns of alcohol use, the individual's learning history with alcohol, and the individual's belief system regarding alcohol, self-control, and other relevant issues (Nathan, 1980; Vaillant, 1983; West, 1984; Royce, 1981).

A number of reasonably well-controlled twin studies have demonstrated a hereditary or genetic component to alcoholism (Bohman, 1978; Rutstein & Veech, 1978; Goodwin, 1976; Goodwin, et al., 1973). In addition, prospective studies (Vaillant, 1983) indicate that the presence of alcoholism in an individual's family is a fairly robust predictor of alcoholism. Further, it is not so much the specificity of an alcoholic relative, (e.g., a father or mother) as it is the number of alcoholic relatives in a given family that best predicts which individuals will have serious alcohol problems.

Regardless of environmental and cultural influences, the frequency of a genotype for alcoholism in an individual's background may mark a predisposition, through unspecified biological processes, toward developing alcohol problems later in life. Clearly, it is advisable to inquire about family history of alcoholism in making decisions regarding early intervention and treatment goals. The greater the family history, the greater the risk of progressive, serious alcohol dependency, and the less likely controlled drinking may be an advisable goal.

Ethnic differences in the incidence of alcohol problems have been recognized for some time. This may point to some cultural and familial patterns of alcohol use that contribute to alcohol problems. In families of Southern European and Mediterranean extraction, where alcohol problems are less prevalent, early socialization regarding alcohol is different from those of Northern European heritage. Southern European families not only use alcohol differently, but differ in the type of beverages used and the tolerance that they espouse for drunkenness. For Southern European and Mediterranean families, alcohol use is ritualized and family centered as opposed to being separate from the family as is typical in Northern European backgrounds (Royce, 1981). The former groups also tend to avoid hard spirits and do not tolerate drunkenness. Again, in Vaillant's (1983) work, Northern European ancestry was a powerful predictor of future problems with alcohol. Nathan (1980) points out that there are not only cultural influences affecting the incidences of alcoholism, but other social conditions as well. Socialization or subcultural variables such as peer pressure, the availability of alcoholic beverages, the demand characteristics of certain settings for heavy drinking, and role models of deviant drinking behavior may further predispose a person to alcohol problems. This *social learning* perspective on drinking suggests that some cultures foster alcoholism through attitudes of acceptance of drunken behavior, denial of the consequences, and the inclusion of drinking as a part of a desirable social role.

Reviews of underlying personality disorders as an etiology for alcoholism cited above have looked into contentions that alcoholics develop their problem drinking as a symptom of some preexisting personality structure. Psychoanalytic theories, for example, often hypothesize a dependent or oral personality, which results in the later development of alcoholism. None of these personality-oriented views have been substantiated. Studies of specific personality traits or characteristics that might discriminate between alcoholics and nonalcoholics prior to the development of alcoholism have generally *not* found positive results (Calahan & Room, 1972; Miller, 1976). Essentially, the various psychological traits that occur in the normal population also occur in alcoholics. Vailant (1983) has pointed out that the presence of alcoholism predicts poor mental health, rather than poor mental health predicting the development of alcoholism. So far, alcoholics have not been found to be premorbidly different from nonalcoholics in personality or overall adjustment, but this does not mean that such differences do not exist. More research is needed.

Treatment approaches that aim at relieving *underlying personality conflicts,* dependent personality traits, or deficits in ego strength as a cure for alcoholic drinking may in themselves be ineffective. However, many emotional, behavioral, and social-adjustment problems no doubt develop as a result of years of alcoholic drinking. The best strategy to address these problems therefore is to eliminate alcohol first and then work on reactive symptoms such as emotional difficulties. In clinical practice, attention had better be given to the problems that have developed over years of drinking, as we shall show in later chapters of this book.

LEARNING THEORY

In general, the broad-based social learning theory described by Bandura (1982) and specifically applied to the problems of alcoholism by Nathan and his associates (Nathan, Titler, Lowenstein, Solomon & Rossi, 1970; Nathan, 1980) can be useful in describing what we know of the etiology of alcoholism. Clearly, becoming psychologically and subsequently physically dependent on alcohol is more than simply a result of the direct chemical effect of the substance. Genetically pre-disposed individuals may well have a greater initial physiological tolerance for alcohol and/or some other deficit in their ability to discriminate their degree of intoxication. They may also be predisposed culturally through their early socialization about alcohol use. In any case, they fail to learn appropriate drinking and/or learn through modeling and other influences a maladaptive pattern of alcohol use that results in their problem drinking. Alcohol abuse leading to psycholo-gical and physical dependence is learned; but not solely through the direct reinforcement that results from the tension reduction that alcohol provides. People's beliefs and expectations about what alcohol will do for them, along with their other irrational cognitions, may well be critical reinforcing variables. Beliefs that alcohol will reduce tension, enhance social effectiveness, and/or prevent emotional discomfort may help people to learn initially and then to maintain their maladaptive drinking.

SUMMARY

The present review of etiological factors in the development of alcoholism suggests that individuals who become troubled by alcohol are *not* necessarily premorbidly different from other people in person-ality traits such as dependence or their psychological adjustment as children. Evidence suggests, however, that they are often premorbidly different in terms of the prevalence of alcoholism in their family history and in their cultural and family patterns regarding alcohol use. Individuals troubled by alcohol, moreover, frequently have a a) specific learning history in which they have developed a psychological reliance upon alcohol as a way of reducing unpleasant emotional experiences or enhancing pleasant ones; b) a long history of heavy alcohol use, despite mounting problems associated with it; and, ultimately, c) a series of conflicting beliefs regarding alcohol, themselves, and other people, which reinforces their habitual and maladaptive use. But just as psychological problems contribute to alcoholism, so too are many psychological, social and vocational problems experienced by alcoholics caused by their alcoholism.

EFFECTIVENESS OF TREATMENT

Miller and Hester (1980) in their review of outcome studies of alcoholism concluded that treatment generally results in about two thirds of the patients improving in the short term, with approximately only one fifth staying improved over the long term. Miller's review, however, provides only the roughest indication of long-term outcome. In addition, treatment in the studies reviewed ranged from residential rehabilitation programs to less intense forms of intervention, but with surprisingly little difference in outcome.

Brandsma (1980), in a review of outpatient treatments, suggests that even though there is significant variability in the types of treatment provided and in the characteristics of the clients treated, treatment is more effective than no intervention. However, this effect tends to attenuate with time. He further points out that essentially all forms of outpatient psychotherapy initially achieve moderate to high degrees of improvement. This finding makes it difficult to discriminate between the relative merits of various treatment approaches, because in general all are found to be *superior* to nontreatment. Brandsma (1980) found similar results in his own comparative study, in which Rational Behavior Therapy (RBT) was compared with attendance at Alcoholics Anonymous, with insight-oriented psychotherapy, and with no treatment controls. The results indicated that all forms of treatment were superior to control conditions, but that only with very sophisticated statistical analysis could the differential effects of various treatment approaches be parsed out.

Again, evidence that treatment works comes from Vaillant's (1983) study. He found that while as many as 20% of alcoholics may have spontaneously remitted or returned to asymptomatic drinking without treatment, those who continued to drink developed more serious alcohol-related problems and did *not* recover without some form of intervention. In this particular study, which spans roughly the years from 1940 to 1980, the most common path to recovery was through participation in Alcoholics Anonymous (AA). (A few individuals who were in psychodynamic, insight-oriented psychotherapy, reported at follow-up that they believed that their participation in this type of psychotherapy actually delayed their recovery because it directed them toward changing their personalities, rather than stopping their drinking.)

No treatment for the seriously addicted drinker can be fatal. Looking at another study reported by Vaillant (1983) in which 100 consecutive admissions to a community alcoholism clinic were studied, severe alcoholics who did not radically change their drinking were likely to die as a direct result of their alcoholism. What Vaillant refers to as the "doctor's dilemma" in the treatment of the severe stages of alcoholism is particularly important. The dilemma is that even the most intensive and costly kind of treatment does not necessarily guarantee recovery. But *no treatment* almost certainly results in *no recovery* and ultimately results in death in many cases. The state of our present knowledge and art is such that we may not be able to "save any given individual alcoholic". However, without intervention that individual will most likely be doomed.

Despite somewhat discouraging results from even the most extensive multimodal and intensive forms of treatment, such as those provided by residential rehabilitation facilities, it is clear that alcoholics can and do recover. How does this happen? What process or processes can facilitate this recovery? As with many other issues concerning alcoholism, there is considerable controversy about the conditions necessary and sufficient for recovery. Clearly, individuals make changes and recover in many ways, (e.g., AA, residential treatment, psychotherapy, prayers, aversive training, a change in life circumstances, and any number of combinations of the above). There is probably no single path to recovery that will apply in all circumstances.

A developmental perspective on recovery, such as suggested by Brown (1985), provides a model for viewing experiences that further recovery in an integrated fashion. Brown argues that *one* of the experiences that can lead to an/or enhance recovery is psychotherapy. Although we differ to some extent with Brown's techniques, we endorse her belief in the value of active, directive, flexible, and cognitive/behavioral therapy for recovery from alcoholism. Therapists need not be pessimistic about the value of treatment after noting that so few alcoholics respond to treatment and that a large number relapse. Psychotherapists often believe that their interventions should produce a "cure" and then prevent the development of future problems. Perhaps we can change our expectations and raise our frustration tolerance. We can accept treatment of alcoholism as helpful.

CONCLUSIONS

In our view, the following practical conclusions are justified by our review of the previously presented information.

1. Alcoholism is multidetermined. There is evidence that predisposing genetic, familial, and cultural factors interact with the individual's social learning history of alcohol use. This results in a pattern of psychological and, in many cases, physical dependence on alcohol. Whether viewed as a disease or behavioral health disorder, alcoholism generally becomes increasingly severe without intervention. Although a variety of treatments may work in a given case, based on the client's characteristics (e.g., age, severity of problem, degree of physical dependence, past history of unsuccessful attempts to change, available social support systems, and preferences) a decision to change and persistent follow-up action on this decision is a prerequisite for arresting the disorder and eventual recovery.

2. Reviews of the outcome literature for both intensive inpatient and outpatient treatment reveal that two out of three cases are "improved" in the short run, but that effectiveness of treatment attenuates with time. Although there is no sure "cure" for alcoholism, particularly when the disorder is severe and well established, lack of treatment or intervention results in further progression with a typically deteriorating course. Persistent trials of therapy may be necessary.

3. Recovery is best seen as a process of change that involves many factors. Psychotherapy that focuses on psychodynamic insight and changing the presumed underlying causes of alcoholism is generally unhelpful. Psychotherapy aimed specifically at helping individuals identify and accept their problem with alcohol, and then to persist in changing their thoughts, feelings, and behaviors that result in pathological alcohol use, does facilitate recovery.

4. RET as a model of human disturbance and a method of helping clients learn to help themselves by stopping drinking and staying stopped, can make an effective and efficient contribution to the development process of an individual's recovery. The decision of an alcoholic to change and the persistence at changing self-defeating thinking about drinking, frustration, and emotional discomfort, along with determination to surrender irrational demands on others, on the world in general, and on themselves, are central to the process of recovery.

Chapter 3
A Rational-Emotive Theory
of Addiction

The purpose of this chapter is to present a model of addictive behavior which will help therapists using RET to develop treatment strategies. As is true of rational-emotive theory in general, we will not present a total theory of the development and etiology of addictive behavior, but rather a theory of symptom maintenance and of *change*. We believe it is safe to assume that the cognitive, behavioral and psychological variables are similar in all addictions, since recent reviews suggest that there are more similarities than differences and that there are common psychological processes to different physiological pressures (Brownell, Marlatt, Lichtenstein, & Wilson (1986); National Institute on Drug Abuse, 1979; Levison, Gerstein, & Maloff, 1983).

ETIOLOGY

It is our belief that the present theories and research data on the etiology of alcoholism and other disorders are not yet sufficiently developed to effectively help therapists plan treatment. Also, theories of etiology can be taken as excuses not to intervene because the hypothesized etiological factors are so "deep," pervasive, or biological (McClearn, 1981; Schuckitt, 1981). Professionals who are working with addicted individuals would benefit by having some hope that their efforts will prove helpful.

BIOLOGICAL FACTORS

There is growing evidence that alcoholism is related to biological (McClearn, 1981; Schuckitt, 1981) and cultural influence (Critchlow, 1986). Some therapists believe that this biological theory of casualty leads logically to pessimism. Rational-emotive theory has always postulated that humans are biological organisms and that frequently, if not always, our psychopathology is routed in our biology (Ellis, 1962, 1973a, 1976b). Perhaps some people are more prone to think irrationally or have a lower threshold for anxiety, depression, anger, or possibly less frustration tolerance and ability for controlling impulses. So, too, with addictions. It is postulated that some people may have biological predispositions to become addicted to various mind-altering substances. The logical implication for such biological causality is not hopelessness but rather the importance of greater effort to overcome the problem. Rational-emotive theory would argue that all behavior is multiply determined and, therefore, clients with strong biological predispositions to a specific problem had better work harder to maximize the influence of psychosocial factors.

If it is true that alcoholics have a strong predisposition to drink or to give in to urges to drink, what are the implications for treatment? RET states that we would expect frequent lapses and relapses. Alcoholics require not only more effort, but possibly more therapy sessions before change occurs. Also we would expect that the efforts to hold back the tide of such biological impulses might be never ending. The clients had better be taught, therefore, not to expect a "cure" (i.e., that desires to drink or use drugs will retire forever). Rather they may expect a lifelong struggle to overcome their problems and had better accept that reality.

BASIC PERSONALITY FLAWS

Most traditional psychotherapy has worked on the assumption that alcoholism and drug abuse is caused by underlying personality problems and that after treating these underlying personality problems the addiction will presumably cease. Vaillant and Milofsky (1982) challenge this notion on two counts. The first is that traditional psychotherapy for addictive behaviors has not worked. In fact, they argue, it may actually have prevented some alcoholics from stopping drinking. The second argument is that many personality problems are a *result of* and not the cause of alcoholism. This notion is accepted by many people in the alcoholism-treatment field. However, recent reanalysis of Vaillant and Milofsky's data (Zucker & Gomberg, 1986) suggests that their methodology is flawed. Specifically, they arranged measurement categories that made it more likely to find no premorbid personality or behavior problems. A reanalysis of Vaillant's data and other studies suggests that early in life people who develop alcoholism displayed problems of impulse control and problems of not conforming to authority.

While research concerning the relationship between early behavior problems and addictive behavior may be helpful in preventing addictions, rational-emotive theory argues that this debate be shelved in favor of treating the client who is currently abusing alcohol or other substances. In clinical practice, we are usually faced with clients who have histories of impulse problems and other personality problems, as well as clients who have failed to mature and develop their personalities as a result of being inebriated for years. The issue of etiology does not have much to do with how to treat them in the beginning stages of therapy nor does it necessarily tell us where to intervene to get them to stop or stay stopped. Treatment will be focused by a theory that explains how the addictive behavior is maintained.

Clients receiving treatment for addictions who had premorbid personality problems are likely to behave in a similar manner in other areas of their lives. If clients cannot control their impulses to drink, they may be likely to give into other self-defeating impulses. A dependent personality who avoids responsibility by resorting to drink is likely to have developed other strategies to avoid life's responsibilities. The rational-emotive therapist will first focus on the irrational beliefs that create and maintain drinking or substance abuse and then focus on the other behavior problems as they emerge, which they usually will. The disturbed behavior patterns that constitute an addictive personality will be manifested in similar irrational thinking. Rational therapists will hope (but not necessarily expect) that giving up one addiction and its corresponding irrationalities will generalize to new rational thinking in other areas of the person's life.

Similarly, if clients have personality problems resulting from having spent years as an addicted person, the rational-emotive therapist will work at both problems—the addiction and the resulting personality problems. For example, a client of ours never learned to overcome his fear of the opposite sex. This may have occurred because he was always high and never learned to desensitize himself to his fear of rejection or develop social skills. We chose not to work first on the inhibited personality problems and hope that eventually the client would stop getting high. Rather, we worked first at eliminating the addiction and then helped the client learn new ways to think about social and sexual relationships by reducing his fears and learning new social skills.

THE IMPORTANCE OF LOW FRUSTRATION TOLERANCE

Rational-emotive theory hypothesizes that irrational beliefs leading to low frustration tolerance will be especially present in addictions. Ellis (1978–1979) has postulated a new affective state he termed *discomfort anxiety* or *discomfort disturbance*. This emotion is the anxiety one feels when anticipating pain, discomfort or unpleasantness. It is usually brought about by the irrational belief that pain, discomfort or unpleasantness is unbearable, and that it cannot and *must* not be tolerated. This belief seems to be almost ubiquitous with people who have addiction problems. We will attempt to identify several different patterns of irrational beliefs, emotions, and behavior that are prevalent in substance abuse.

Low-Frustration Tolerance-Blocking Abstinence

The primary cognitive dynamic that creates and maintains addiction is what we call the abstinence LFT pattern (Fig. 3.1). Most people with impulse-control problems fit into this pattern regardless of the substance or action to which they are addicted. For example, they can overindulge in alcohol, food, heroin, cocaine, marijuana, pills, gambling, sex, or love.

The dynamic pattern usually starts when people first encounter stimulus cues that elicit a desire for self-destructive addictive behavior. The cue could be the smell of pastry baking, passing an off-track betting parlor, or being with one's drinking buddies. Clients may then decide whether or not to partake. The decision not to consume the desired addictive substance is the Activating Event in the ABCs. The temporary deprivation resulting from this decision to abstain is then followed by low frustration tolerance stemming from irrational beliefs. These may be:

- I cannot stand avoiding a drink.
- I cannot function without a drink.
- I am not strong enough to resist alcohol.
- I cannot stand the deprivation of my desire for a drink.
- I am a horribly deprived person if I cannot have a drink.
- Life is too hard so I am entitled to have a drink.
- To make up for my difficult life, I must have a drink.
- I must have a drink or I can't go on.
- I must not abstain when it's so enjoyable to imbibe.
- I must not abstain when it is so painful to do so.

These irrational beliefs lead to the emotional disturbance of low-frustration tolerance (LFT) or discomfort anxiety in the ABC paradigm. Clients overcome this LFT in several ways:

1. They can wait for the urges for the desired substance to pass. Since they have such a childish demand for comfort, this is unlikely.

E-RET—C

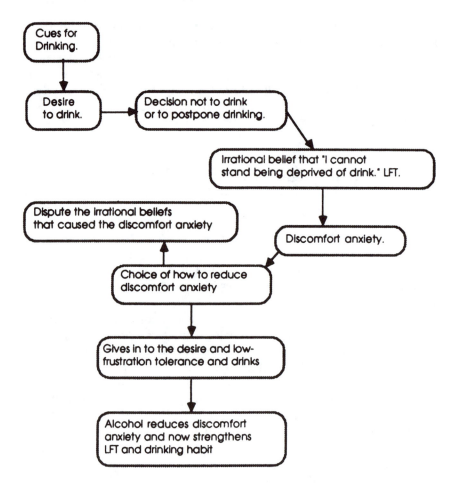

FIGURE 3.1. The Abstinence and LFT Pattern

2. They can dispute the irrational beliefs that cause the discomfort anxiety. Again, this is hard work and will require some pain until the process of disputing actually changes the disturbed emotion.
3. They can quickly and immediately remove the discomfort anxiety by giving in to the impulse and eliminating the activating event—the imagined or actual deprivation.

Regardless of how the addiction started, this pattern is sufficient to keep it going.

The reason addictions are too easy to create and maintain is that no cognitive or behavioral strategy can eliminate the discomfort anxiety as quickly and as effortlessly as chemicals. All other strategies, (i.e., philosophical disputing, cognitive distraction, coping self-statements, stimulus control, practicing an incompatible behavior) require some time to work. During that time, the addict experiences the discomfort. Also, all strategies other than indulging in the addiction require effort—which is the one thing that people with low-frustration tolerance don't take to very well!

PROBLEMS IN IDENTIFYING THE ABSTINENCE → LFT PATTERN

Although the abstinence → LFT dynamic appears easy to understand, therapists learning RET frequently ignore this pattern in their efforts to change addictive behavior. Our supervision experience in training therapists in RET suggests that most professionals new to RET miss this point. There are two reasons for this misdiagnosis.

Ellis (1978–1979) created the term discomfort anxiety precisely because the affect that results from low-frustration-tolerance cognitions is so difficult to label in English. Try the following exercise to understand this point. Pick your most prevalent addiction or obsession, such as food, liquor, or cigarettes. Now try to imagine all the enjoyment you would get from indulging in that substance. Now tell yourself how unbearable it would be to deprive yourself of it. Really *whine* about it. Now try to label the emotion. What is it called? Having observed hundreds of therapists and clients do this exercise, we have noticed how difficult it is for people to label this affective state. What do we call this feeling that occurs when we demand that we *must* fulfill our addictive desire, yet we decide to or are forced into being deprived of it? Some call it craving others call it deprivation, agitation, or panic. Most people report it is a negative and disturbing feeling, whatever term they use. Ellis uses the term *discomfort anxiety*. We would hypothesize that this semantic hole makes it difficult for clients to label the feeling from which they are escaping when they indulge in addictive behavior. If clients cannot label and therefore do not report this upsetting emotion, the therapist is unlikely to investigate the irrational beliefs that create it.

Another reason novice therapists miss this cognitive dynamic is the strategy they use to question clients. When clients report having used or abused a substance, the RET practitioner looks for the ABCs before disputing. The therapist asks the clients how they are feeling. Because the clients have already imbibed the intoxicant, they are feeling okay—or feeling guilt or remorse over the transgression. The feeling of discomfort anxiety has passed. Clients are likely to want fast relief from their discomfort anxiety, so they don't feel it too long. In fact they usually get high as soon as the urge occurs so they can avoid feeling any discomfort anxiety. Clients then say they feel guilty about drinking and the therapist looks for and disputes their irrational ideas that lead to guilt. It is not necessarily bad to dispute the irrational beliefs that lead to guilt, as we shall discuss below. However, this strategy does not get to the core problems, and it could result in the client's not even feeling remorse over the drinking episode.

Techniques for Uncovering LFT

There are several ways to discover whether the abstinence LFT dynamic is present. Talk with clients about what they feel when they deprive themselves of their addiction, or ask them how they feel when they are in a situation where they can't drink or alcohol is unavailable to them. They will resist, look blank, shrug their shoulders—but you keep fishing.

Try to establish their words for discomfort anxiety. Teach them to label this feeling. Ask them to imagine they are presented with their favorite intoxicant and they are trying not to use it. Let them keep imagining it is there and let the desire and whining for it continue. That is discomfort anxiety.

The next time these clients report they have drunk, snorted, popped, shot up, or smoked, ask them how they felt just before they gave into the urge. What were they thinking just before they gave in? Then you can focus on disputing as well as teaching them how they can think and feel differently.

INTOXICATION AS COPING

Another common cognitive dynamic pattern is drinking alcohol (or getting high on other substances) to avoid or to escape from problems. This leads to intoxication as coping (Fig. 3.2). Alcohol has always been noted for its relaxing effects. The cultural expectation is that it will reduce tension. The busy executive is expected to have a drink or two to unwind after a day at the office. Marijuana is also expected to "mellow out" those who have to relax. Despite the widespread cultural belief that alcohol, marijuana and other drugs are relaxants, and although such drugs do bring about some of the physiological responses of

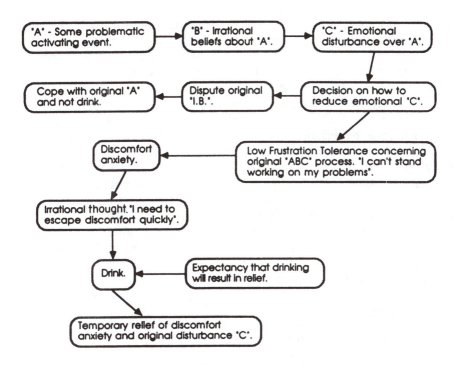

FIGURE 3.2. The 'Intoxication as Coping' Pattern

relaxation, the effects of these substances are not always consistent with the physiological effects of relaxation.

For example, alcohol is perceived as a relaxation-producing substance, yet one of its physiological effects is to increase heart rate, which is the exact opposite of what happens in relaxation. The alcoholics are actually deluding themselves that alcohol is a good way to unwind. However, they may feel partly relaxed as a result of drinking and fail to learn a better way to relax. The same can be said of other substances, except for drugs designed as antianxiety medications such as Valium and Xanex. Those who are addicted to this class of drugs truly have a chemical form of relaxing.

Rational-emotive therapy teaches people that they can change their disturbing emotions by identifying and challenging their irrational beliefs whenever they make themselves upset. Although we believe RET to be a highly efficient form of therapy, it usually doesn't work immediately. In order to make therapy work, clients have to practice their coping skills when they feel upset. This means that they are usually already in some emotional discomfort before they try coping.

This is where rational-emotive theory hypothesizes that most persons with addictive disorders have their worst problem. They refuse to allow themselves to be uncomfortable long enough to learn effective coping strategies. In effect, the emotional disturbance they experience at point C in the ABCs of RET, becomes an Activating Event for a new set of irrational beliefs and a new emotional problem. Rational-emotive therapy calls this process of upset leading to irrational beliefs and more upset *symptom stress* or *secondary emotional disturbance* (Walen, DiGiuseppe, & Wessler, 1980). In clients with addictive disorders, symptom stress appears to be pervasive. They do not tolerate the feelings of depression, anxiety, hurt or rage that they feel. When they experience such disturbed emotions, they think irrational thoughts about their disturbances. Some examples of their irrational beliefs that create discomfort anxiety or low frustration tolerance about their original anxiety, depression, or rage are:

- I can't stand being upset.
- I must be emotionally happy.
- I must not experience the hassles of having emotional problems.
- I must not be upset.
- I'm not supposed to be upset.
- I'm too weak to stand this upsetting emotion.

These irrational beliefs then lead to discomfort anxiety. Alcoholics or addicted clients can avoid their discomfort anxiety by disputing the irrational beliefs leading to it. However, the quickest and easiest way to remove discomfort anxiety, they soon see and come to expect, is to become intoxicated. This not only ends the secondary discomfort anxiety, but the original upsetting emotion that started the symptom. Stress serves as a negative reinforcer, which will also, therefore, increase the likelihood that the behavior will occur again in the future.

It is important to note that in the "intoxication as coping" model, the drugs or alcohol may not be positively reinforcing. Clients may not get high because they enjoy the sensation they experience when high. Actually, they experience a kind of negative reinforcement process operating here. The reinforcement for using intoxicants is the removal of pain. In this case, the removal of the emotional pain and upset they experienced about the original activating events as well as the removal of the symptom stress serves as a negative reinforcer that will therefore increase the likelihood that the behavior will occur again in the future.

The fact that one uses alcohol or drugs not for pleasure but rather for the removal of pain may seem strange at first. After all, few substance abusers will admit that they use drugs and alcohol for such purposes.

They refer to their drinking as "partying" and use other gala phrases to describe their addiction in terms that indicate a good time. However, a behavioral analysis of a particular client's use pattern may indicate alcohol or drug use each time the client faces an upsetting situation or is under pressure to perform. Marlatt's (1983) research indicates that most substance abusers relapse when confronted with emotionally upsetting situations. Frequently, clients may report that they use drugs to feel numb or just to escape. Drug use, therefore, serves a negatively reinforcing purpose. It helps them to avoid or escape discomfort in the short run.

Using alcohol or other intoxicants to relieve the discomfort of original anxiety and of symptom stress has several negative effects: (a) it reinforces clients' beliefs that they cannot stand emotional discomfort; (b) it reinforces the habit of drinking in order to solve emotional problems; (c) it reinforces the habit of responding to problematic activating events with intoxication; and (d) it prevents the client from learning other effective coping strategies for problematic Activating Events. This last outcome can be most debilitating because it prevents the alcoholic from coping or dealing with life problems. Thus, clients may avoid areas of functioning and fail to develop competencies they could have otherwise developed.

We believe that this mechanism may account for Vaillant's (1983) notion that alcoholism often leads to personality disorders. For example, clients believe that they cannot stand the hassles of interpersonal negotiation and therefore drink every time they become upset negotiating with their spouses. As a result, they do not resolve any of the emotional issues in their relationships. With time, they become emotionally and socially isolated. If the marriages end, they may be unable to develop relationships with new partners. These clients become isolated and may appear schizoid because of their failures to learn how to negotiate and compromise in a relationship. Because people rarely learn when high, being frequently inebriated will eventually deprive them of the knowledge and experience that make up what we call maturity. In addition, the brain injury suffered by many confirmed alcoholics will cause them to think *more* irrationally than they did when they first took to drinking.

Difficulties Uncovering the Intoxication as Coping Pattern

Perhaps the greatest problem in identifying the underlying irrational beliefs in addicts is their tendency to deny the problem. Therapists and family members often think they understand the denial because they have named it. The intoxication as coping model *explains* how denial operates. Denial can be maintained not only because the drug- and alcohol-abusing clients are cognitively distorting reality, but also because they *view* themselves as having no problem. These clients experience no problem because their lack of frustration tolerance and quick escape by drinking results in their avoiding any discomfort. They escape into a stupor at the first inkling of negative feelings. Thus, they are not denying a problem; they actually don't *experience* one. Addicts fail to develop many competencies, but because of denial, they continue to "function". They falsely see themselves as functioning well in areas where they are really incompetent.

The alcohol- and drug-abuse literature ubiquitously refers to the presence of family members who help the addicted persons avoid their problems—the enablers. The presence of an enabler will again help alcoholics to avoid recognizing their problems. But denial is not really a good term for the addict's failure to see a problem. The enabler actually fixes many problems that result from the abuser's indulgence so that there is no problem to be seen!

RET therapists may not have to deal with the alcoholic's denial because what is labeled "denial" is really faulty perception. More usefully, the clinician had better break through the distortions caused by the discomfort anxiety and its avoidance and help alcoholics see the real difficulties that are removed by the "help" of enablers.

Techniques for Uncovering the Intoxication as Coping Pattern

One effective way to have alcoholic and drug-using clients become aware of their failure to cope with problems is by having the enabler resign from the role. Once this happens, many of the errors and difficulties clients have been able to avoid start to pile up. The initial reaction by clients may be to act indifferently. After all, they may be unaware of exactly how much the enabler has protected them. Then the problem drinking is likely to worsen. As the enabler withdraws, the number of problems or unpleasant Activating Events will likely increase and the drinker will no longer be protected from them. As the problems increase, the clients will tend to respond to the emotional consequences with their usual solution—intoxication. Thus, the amount of time spent intoxicated is likely to increase. As the clients are increasingly intoxicated, more things in life will go unattended and as a result more unpleasant Activating Events will occur. Finally, clients will tend to be overwhelmed by the number of problems. They may lose a job, a place to live, be alone, not have food, or be in jail. Then they cannot escape by intoxication and may admit there really is a problem.

This strategy may actually precipitate a crisis. The crisis generally overwhelms the addicts with problems, so they become aware of their inadequacy in coping. Precipitating a crisis can only be accomplished if the enablers give up what they intend to be helpful roles. But as the problems mount, these enablers may be drawn into a Messiah role by their own irrational beliefs. The crisis may only be precipitated and managed if a therapist works with the enabler to prevent a rescue. The treatment of enablers will be discussed more in Chapter 10.

Not all clients are so addicted that they will require a crisis before they admit their problems. There are several other strategies clinicians can use to help them become aware of their demands for comfort. One strategy is to review the episodes of drinking that have occurred recently. If they have occurred in relation to problematic Activating Events and it appears intoxication was used for coping, further questioning is warranted. Imagine that clients experienced Activating Events without any access to alcohol or drugs. How would they be feeling? What would they be thinking? Also focus on what they would feel and think about any emotional disturbance elicited by the Activating Event and the irrational beliefs that they would hold about it.

An additional strategy focuses on admitted failures. Try to find out what clients' major practical problems are. Perhaps their job doesn't pay enough; they haven't finished school; they hate to attend class or take exams. Then focus on why these problems haven't been solved and what could have been done to resolve them. Once the clients have admitted that there are solutions to their practical problems, turn the questioning to what stops them from following through on these solutions. What would they feel if they attempted the solutions? Frequently clients will still be unaware of their problems and you may suggest to them that Low Frustration Tolerance stops them from attempting to select or to reach a goal. You may point out how their complaints are inconsistent with their lack of effort to overcome their practical problems and then forcefully point out how they may be avoiding solutions because of discomfort anxiety.

INTOXICATION EQUALS
WORTHLESSNESS

Many alcoholics and drug users believe they are hopelessly caught in a pattern of behavior from which they cannot escape. Once they accept themselves as users, abusers, or addicts, they also may easily rate themselves as worthless human beings. This thinking leads to guilt and depression. The clients drink or abuse drugs to relieve the depression; then the clients once again condemn themselves for their addiction. Not all those suffering from addictive disorders fit this pattern, but a substantial portion fit what we call the "Intoxication Equals Worthlessness" pattern. This pattern is outlined in Figure 3.3.

Once these individuals sober up from a drinking episode, they are often confronted by the negative consequences of their binge, such as

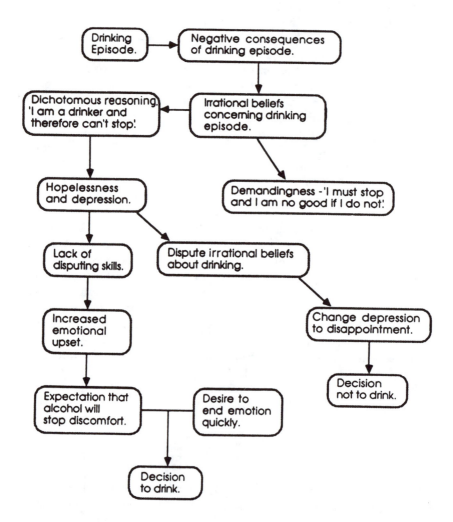

FIGURE 3.3. The 'Intoxication Equals Worthlessness' Pattern

the work they missed, the school assignments not done, the classes cut, the appointments forgotten, the insults delivered. Now they can choose to accept themselves for having made serious errors and forgive themselves for the transgressions that followed their indulgence, or they can condemn themselves for what they have done. Many alcoholics and drug users who have basically neurotic personalities use each episode of substance abuse as an opportunity to castigate themselves. The irrational beliefs likely to occur in this cognitive dynamic are of two types. The first is the absolute demand that under all conditions drug abuse should not have occurred in the past and must not occur now or in the future. Because these clients have not lived up to this dogmatic demand, they deduce that they are worthless people. The worthlessness follows from the demandingness.

The second type of irrationality involves dichotomous reasoning. Addicted persons will identify themselves as being either users or nonusers. If they drink one drop—or take one hit of a joint or one snort of cocaine—they are users. The line between a user and nonuser is exact, rigid, and inflexible. Thus, when these individuals try to stop, they are at risk. While they are abstaining, they are nonusers. Once they take one bit of their addicted substance, they are abusers. Once they label themselves as abusers, they have defined themselves as unable to stop. Marlatt and Gordon (1985) review considerable research and clinical material to indicate how this dichotomous reasoning or labelling increases the likelihood that a small lapse by an addict will result in a total relapse. They call this the *abstinence violation effect* (AVE) because the one-time violation of abstinence is seen as a total relapse. This definition of oneself as an abuser can lead to a belief in one's hopelessness and one's helplessness to escape from the addiction.

THE DEMAND FOR EXCITEMENT

For over 25 years, researchers have been noticing a relationship between alcoholism and psychopathy (Glueck & Glueck, 1950; McCord & McCord 1960). Some researchers believe that psychopathy is primary and leads to alcoholism (Robins, 1966), whereas others think that psychopathic symptoms develop from alcoholism (Vaillant, 1980). Schuckitt (1973) believes that these are not mutually exclusive categories and that two possibilities exist to explain the frequently found link between alcoholism and psychopathy: (a) that alcohol and drug abuse is but one symptom of an underlying antisocial personality, and (b) that alcohol and drug abusers manifest antisocial symptoms as a consequence of the primary dependency. Vaillant (1983) has found that members of his sample of alcoholics fall into both categories. Thus it appears likely that any clinician working with alcoholics and substance abusers will be confronted with clients who are often psychopathic.

If some alcoholics and drug abusers are primarily psychopaths, what is the mechanism to account for psychopathy leading to substance abuse? Several theorists have noted that psychopaths appear to have high levels of desire for excitement or stimulation as well as poor impulse control (Cleckley, 1982; Hare, 1986). Rational-emotive theory hypothesizes that the high sensation seeking of psychopaths is not sufficient to lead them to drink. However, if high sensation seeking is coupled with psychopaths' holding of the irrational belief that they cannot stand or tolerate boredom or monotony, trouble will result. Such a combination can lead to disturbed discomfort anxiety when stimulation is minimal, due to their low tolerance for boredom. Add to this the expectation that drugs or drink will provide a good time, and the psychopath will be more likely to drink or use drugs. This pattern of thoughts and feelings is diagramed in Figure 3.4. The rational-emotive

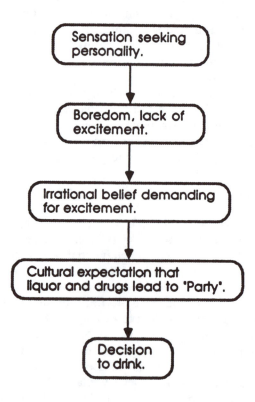

FIGURE 3.4. The Demand for Excitement Pattern

therapist would first attempt the philosophical solution of disputing the addicted psychopath's demand that life always be exciting and help them accept that they can tolerate routine activities, boredom, and everyday life. Empirical strategies could help them learn less destructive ways of satisfying their sensation-seeking urges and help them conceptualize that not *only* good times and fun are the consequences of drinking and drug use, but that bad things have happened to them as well.

Chapter 4
General Treatment Considerations

This chapter will review a number of general treatment issues that are important considerations in RET with alcohol-troubled clients. RET is best practiced when it is understood that theory alone, regardless of how elegant or pragmatically descriptive, does not necessarily result in favorable therapeutic outcomes. Persistent and energetic action following from the theory is most likely to lead to change. In working with alcoholics, this is particularly important.

Often individuals with alcohol problems know, in an intellectual way, that they ought to change in order to stop experiencing their difficulties, but for rather complex reasons they are not able to do so. Effective RET with such clients, then, does not simply involve helping them to identify dysfunctional thoughts but also provides them with a series of quite specific techniques and experiences that will help them change their thoughts, feelings and actions as they relate not only to alcohol use but also as they relate to the problems of everyday living. Sweeping generalizations about the only proper way to treat individuals with alcohol or other substance-abuse problems are better avoided. Whenever specific suggestions are made, it is prudent for the practicing therapist to determine in each individual case to what extent these may apply.

INITIATING TREATMENT

RET, like all forms of psychotherapy, occurs within the context of an interpersonal relationship. Specific qualities or characteristics of this relationship are viewed as neither necessary nor sufficient for change in and of themselves. Relationship issues do have a bearing, however, on the degree to which a client is likely to be persuaded to undertake specific efforts to change. Without some degree of alliance between therapist and client, the sustained effort required to change strong habits is less likely to occur.

Individuals who are troubled by alcohol and other drug problems have often been told by people in their lives that they need to change. Despite their "knowledge" that change would be in their best interest, they have not acted effectively. RET involves establishing a relationship in which clients are encouraged and reinforced for honestly sharing their thoughts and feelings as well as accurately reporting their behavior so that emotional insight and specific action results. Depending upon the characteristics of the client, including their past experiences with intervention and their present conception of their difficulties, the initiation of effective treatment may require considerable time and effort on the part of the therapist.

The RET practice literature (e.g., Walen, DiGiuseppe, & Wessler, 1980; Wessler & Wessler, 1980) suggests that clients are more likely to be open to a persuasive and directive approach such as RET when they have established trust and confidence in the therapist. Rational-emotive therapy posits that the therapeutic relationship is based on the following: (a) an unconditional acceptance of the client by the therapist, (b) the demonstration that the therapist will actively work at understanding the client, and (c) the demonstration that the therapist will work at helping the client change. Proceeding in an active-directive manner communicates to the client the therapist's caring as well as the therapist's concern that the client stop suffering. With some alcoholics, particularly those who have relapsed frequently, specific attention to the above considerations is important. The therapist-client relationship in RET encourages trust, positive expectations, confidence in the expertise of the therapist, and acceptance of clients despite their problems. In this atmosphere, the clients are more likely to share their private thoughts, feelings and actions. Decision making, goal setting and, most importantly, responsibility for progress toward these goals can be shared. The greatest barrier to forming such a therapeutic relationship may be the irrationality of the therapist (Ellis, 1985a). It is easy to succumb to one's own LFT or "dire need" for achievement with clients who frequently relapse. By stubbornly refusing to condemn the clients for their failures or demanding a positive response to treatment, the therapist is more likely to build a sound relationship.

ESTABLISHING A COLLABORATIVE RELATIONSHIP

The initial sessions with an alcoholic client can be directed toward clarifying self-identification of the problem, beginning to assess the dimensions of the client's alcoholism and, most importantly, establishing a collaborative relationship. Although most therapists attempt to build a working relationship with clients by active listening and reflection, rational-emotive theory suggests that these are only some possible techniques that can be used to promote an effective therapeutic relationship. More important, in our view, is the therapist's consistent effort over time to demonstrate acceptance of individual clients as people, even when problems of alcohol or substance abuse exists.

Also critical is the therapist's active involvement in attempting to understand the client and help initiate change. Seeking detailed information, sharing hypotheses about the client, and suggesting specific change strategies demonstrates to the client that the therapist is actively involved in helping.

Certainly by listening but also by questioning, commenting and directly teaching, the therapist becomes involved with the clients and their problems. This involvement also demonstrates that therapy will be a collaborative effort. Change will come from the active efforts of both client and therapist. Although the problems presented by clients are certainly difficult, there is no evidence that they are "too hard" if you work on them together. Most alcoholics and substance abusers have tried to change on their own with little or no success. By credibly demonstrating that change will come from your joint efforts, you can help establish realistic but positive expectations about the change process. Though there is no magical cure for the client's myriad problems, such active and collaborative involvement helps establish the belief on the client's part that change is possible.

AVOID GENERALIZATIONS

The credibility and trust implicit in the development of a therapeutic relationship is not well served by making premature assumptions or generalizations about the client's problems with alcohol or other substances. Statements about all alcoholics or substance abusers having a given personality or trait or dysfunctional family background not only fail the tests of reason and evidence but also can be construed by clients as negative judgments or put-downs. While clinical experience and research can provide guidance about the common problems often associated with drug and alcohol abuse, encouraging clients to tell you about themselves through the judicious use of questions and dialogue provides the most helpful avenue to change. It is the client's view of the problem at hand that is crucial. Regardless of how inaccurate, uninformed, illogical or distorted the client's beliefs might be, the long-term process of change is clearly better served by changing those beliefs than by changing dogmatically held generalizations about all alcoholics or substance abusers.

In our experience in giving professional workshops, we will often hear generalizations from therapists such as "alcoholics lack motivation for treatment" or "clients with addictive personalities are resistant and do not really want help". This population of clients may well be frustrating for many therapists but there is no evidence to support such generalizations. Clearly, therapists who hold such views dogmatically may do considerable harm in working with this population, and clients would be better served if they did not. Moreover, the overt or covert communication of such irrationality does nothing to promote the kind of effective therapeutic relationship we have been describing. It biases the therapist toward negative expectations and pessimism, rather than active and persistent effort. Further, such generalizations contradict the total acceptance of the client, problems and all, which you had better try to communicate. Clearly, if you cannot really accept such clients, problems and all, you had better work on this issue yourself before treating them.

IDENTIFYING KEY PROBLEMS

Effective and efficient RET requires specific effort to identify problems of significance to the client even in the initial sessions. Questions such as "What problem do you want help with? " can provide information toward a definition of these key problems. Questions such as "Why are you here now? " or "What would you like help with at this time? " can also assist in defining the therapeutic relationship as one in which help is sought and provided about specific and timely issues of immediate practical concern to the client. The process of defining these key concerns can also provide very useful information about the clients' views of their problems with alcohol or other substances. While problems identified initially might only be the tip of the iceberg, the process of asking such questions and taking their answers seriously within the clients' frames of reference establishes some initial roles for the relationship. You, as therapist, are actively interested in client's views of the problem and will persistently encourage them to explore, define, and ultimately change these views so that long-term and lasting progress can be achieved.

E-RET—D

In answer to initial questions regarding what help the client desires at this time, much useful information may emerge. For example, the client may say "My wife thinks I drink too much". This can be followed up with a dialogue to redirect the client's attention toward what he thinks about his drinking, how much is too much, what happens when he drinks, and so forth. This can establish the therapeutic alliance by pointing out to the client that what he or she thinks about the problem is more important that what others think. The emphasis here is on establishing a locus of control for defining problems within the client as the first step in solving these problems.

It is probably unwise, even in the interest of establishing rapport with a reluctant client, to agree with that client's definition of her or his problem as residing in someone or something else. This might encourage the client to evolve self-defeating expectations and goals for therapy. In the example above, the client might wish to gain from therapy a change in his wife's attitude about his drinking (i.e., her becoming more tolerant of it). This might result in wasted time and effort as well as continued problems with substance abuse for the client. It is important for the therapist not only to be concerned about rapport and to avoid being judgmental but also from the outset to correct misconceptions and misunderstandings about the purpose of therapy.

A SELF-HELP ORIENTATION

While establishing appropriate and therapeutic expectations through active involvement with the client and specific dialogue to define key client problems, it is also important to teach the client about RET's self-help orientation. From the outset the client will be expected to work at change in a prescribed manner in order to make progress.

While you as the therapist have a plan to guide clients' efforts and will stay actively involved and accept them as people, they will get little out of the relationship by waiting passively for you to "cure" them. While it is not helpful to say to clients in so many words, "You have to do it on your own," it is equally self-defeating to say to them, "I'll do it all for you." If they could have changed on their own, they probably would not have come to see you; and likewise, if you had discovered a cure for alcoholism or substance abuse, you would not be earning your living seeing one client at a time, since you would be too busy collecting the Nobel Prize for your discovery.

It is most efficient to teach clients your self-help orientation in a direct didactic manner. This can be done by saying something along the lines of the following:

I spend my professional life teaching people about how they can change the way they think, feel and act. In doing this, one thing I've learned is that I can't make people change. I just don't have that kind of magic or power. But I've also found out in a great number of cases somewhat like yours that people can change themselves once they learn how to do so and really work at it. In order for me to teach you how to help yourself, I will from time to time suggest that you do certain assignments. I will ask you to keep records of your thoughts, feelings, and actions between our visits, read helpful books or listen to tapes, including tapes of our work together. In doing these activities or maybe some others that we will devise together, you'll practice changing the behavior patterns that are getting you in a jam. I think you'll find that, while this may seem to be a nuisance, it really pays off in the long run. You don't have to do these assignments, but if you do I'm pretty sure you will get better faster.

Of course, not all clients will get your message when so directly presented, but the same ideas can be presented in less direct ways and can also be discussed on other occasions during your work together. Some alcoholics and substance abusers seem to go to great lengths to prove that "it's my life and nobody is going to tell me what to do". The only point worth making here is that if clients want certain negative consequences in their lives to change, then they will do well to consider your suggestions. In the final analysis, all forms of therapy or healing are self-help.

CREATING POSITIVE EXPECTATIONS AND SETTING LIMITS

In initiating therapy, pay some attention to creating realistic expectations by the client and to defining the limits of the services to be provided. It is useful first to find out what the client's expectations are regarding change by asking questions like "What have you tried to do about your drinking in the past? " Alcoholic clients have often decided to change many times in the past and may well have also promised to significant others that they would change. They may have even been successful in undertaking some limited change for a period of time. Unfortunately, this change has not endured.

This discussion provides an opportunity to point out that not only is desire to change required but also that persistent action and some hard work will be required to maintain this change. Many clients believe incorrectly that because they have come to understand their problem in relatively simple terms—for example "I need to stop or cut down my drinking"—that this simple understanding should result in some easy solution to their problem. As we often point out, *simple* and *easy* are not synonymous. It's rarely easy to change automatic, habitual, noncon-scious and relatively longstanding patterns of thinking, feeling, and acting. In this context it can be useful to discuss the clients' past efforts at change. A simple model in terms of the rational-emotive psychology of addiction can be used to illustrate why change is not easy and why they have encountered such difficulties in the past.

Related to clients' expectations is the establishment of specific limitations for the therapy. Drug- and alcohol-abusing clients may expect a great deal from therapists and you may have to set limits on your availability and their attendance. Our experience is that many substance abusers have repeated crises in their lives when they relapse, abuse, or first remain dry. Even in the interest of rapport it is clearly unwise to tell a client to call you if they "have any problems," if you are unwilling or unlikely to be available. It would be damaging to the therapeutic alliance for the therapist to fail to deliver on a promise.

Consistent with the decision-making focus of RET and the mainte-nance of a self-help orientation it is important to clear up such practical issues initially. People who abuse mind-altering drugs often have poor judgment and impulse control and will attempt to lean on others to address the negative consequences of the fallout. One can view limit setting in terms of opportunities to address issues of irrational beliefs that lead to irresponsible behavior. Their choosing not to live by established procedures and limits may result in their calling at three in the morning at the scene of a car accident caused by their drinking. They will have strong feelings of dependency if you help them and anger if you don't. Clients' feelings and thoughts about you for setting limits are grist for the therapeutic mill, as is the generation of problem-solving strategies to guide clients when they are tempted to violate the limits of therapy.

At the Institute for RET in New York and in our independent practices, we give our clients a written description of our practice procedures and policies, our times available, and telephone policies in order to clarify the limits we have been discussing.

ASSESSMENT ISSUES

Assessment of clients with specific alcohol and substance-abuse problems is an important part of initial stages of treatment and is often essential to effective treatment planning. However, in RET the assess-ment process is different from the traditional assessment with formal psychometric or psychodiagnostic testing. In RET assessment is a systematic, clinical process aimed at understanding the client's self-defeating cycles of thought, feeling, and action. Also, assessment in RET is an ongoing process. It is not something set apart and conducted only in the initial sessions or through some formal history taking. Rather it is seen as a hypothesis-generating and testing process.

Relevant information is collected by the clinician. Hypotheses are generated about specific dysfunctional ideas and their consequent emotions and behaviors; and then further questions are asked and data collected from the client to confirm or disconfirm these hypotheses. If the clinician's hypotheses are disconfirmed, new ones are formed and the process continues.

We prefer to begin this hypothesis-testing method of assessment with the first question in the first session. This question, namely, "What problem would you like help with at this time? " then leads to further dialogue that specifies the problem in terms of its severity, duration, and related complications. We believe this type of assessment goes hand-in-hand with the establishment of rapport, reasonable expectations, and a therapeutic alliance, because clients see that the therapist is actively engaged in attempting to understand them. This approach to assessment shows and models for the clients how logic and data can be used to uncover and test faulty cognitions——a process they will be taught to apply in overcoming their own problems.

Referral information is an excellent but often-disregarded source of initial assessment information and hypotheses. The historical information that most therapists collect as part of assessment, we believe, is best collected by paper-and-pencil questionnaire either before the first session or between the first two sessions. This information can be useful in generating hypotheses regarding the client's presenting complaints. Historical information such as age, vocational and marital status, sex, referral source and previous treatment experiences can be most informative. Based on what we've previously discussed about the "natural history" of alcoholism, merely knowing these few facts may generate some hypotheses with which to direct dialogue in the initial sessions. In addition, as a therapist, your familiarity with the characteristics of your treatment setting or practice can also generate some assessment hypotheses. Although the demands for specific record keeping and report writing in a given treatment setting may require more formalized assessment, it is our view that assessment is to be thought out formally but need not be a formidable undertaking.

HISTORY OF SUBSTANCE ABUSE

Because of the multidimensional nature of alcoholism and related substance-abuse problems, as well as alcoholic individuals' tendency to fail to see a connection between their drinking and its consequences, some assessment of the client's history of alcohol abuse is generally useful. It is best to be thorough so as not to miss important medical, social, family or vocational complications, but you need not take an exhaustive history. Although a number of formal assessment devices as well as computer-generated scales to take these histories are available, it is our finding that a clinical history of the client's problems with alcohol is probably sufficient for our purposes. First of all, it allows the therapist to gauge the severity of the presenting problem with alcohol for use in hypothesis generation and treatment goal setting. Second, it informs the client that therapy will be concerned with addressing the present cause of these problems—namely, the client's self-defeating habits with alcohol rather than other issues. Further, through this process, clients can be given another way of objectifying their concern with these problems, which can help them in overcoming their tendency to see their problems as unrelated to drinking. Knowing what kind of trouble alcohol and drugs have caused your clients can also be used later in treatment to remind them of the costs of its misuse. This can help the therapeutic process back on track and allow the therapist to more vividly and forcefully dispute with clients their irrational ideas about alcohol use.

In taking a history of alcohol- or drug-related problems, it is helpful to be as specific yet as nonjudgmental as possible. Questions such as "How much do you drink? " might be better framed as "When was the last time you had a drink? " Legal problems resulting from use might be assessed by asking: "Have you ever been stopped for drinking and driving? " Family and/or marital problems from use can be probed by asking "Have your wife/husband or kids ever told you that you drink too much? " Other questions such as "Has your doctor ever told you to stop or cut down on your drinking? " may lead to a series of related questions about health issues. Economic or vocational issues can be assessed with questions like "Do you ever go to work with a hangover?" or more specifically, "Have you ever been fired or told your job was in danger due to your drinking? " Problems with control and/or the perception of control can be assessed with questions such as "Do you ever drink more than you intended once you began to drink?" or "Have you ever tried to stop drinking and found it hard or impossible to do? "

The above questions are samples of those that can be used to guide the clinician in assessing the social, economic, legal, interpersonal, and personal consequences of excessive substance use. The novice clinician or the clinician inexperienced with alcoholism and substance-abuse problems can productively refer to Vaillant's (1983) Problem Drinking Scale, the Michigan Alcoholism Screening Test (Seilzer, 1971) or the

Vogler and Bartz (1982) Drinking Survey for specific protocols that can be useful in developing a personal style for taking such a history. Once again, the purpose of such a history is not for research or definitive diagnosis but rather to collect information about the consequences of alcohol or substance abuse for a given individual.

COGNITIVE ASSESSMENT

In addition to assessing the individual's problems with alcohol, the most crucial aspect of the initial assessment is to specify the dysfunctional cognitions, irrational beliefs, and disruptive emotions that the client experiences and which are maintaining the self-defeating pattern of substance abuse. In chapters 5, 6 and 9 we will discuss in considerable detail some of these irrational ideas and their emotional consequences as they apply to many alcoholics. Our combined clinical experience suggests that certain irrational beliefs are more prevalent in alcoholics and that they prevent therapy from really starting. The clinician may well look for statements that can be used to steer the substance abuser away from treatment.

The following is a constellation of problematic beliefs: First, you can anticipate a significant amount of symptom stress with many alcoholics. You had better therefore listen for self-damnation and self-pity for having the problem in the first place. Second are problems with discomfort anxiety and low frustration tolerance. The beliefs that changing their pattern of alcohol misuse is "too hard" and/or will result in overwhelming levels of discomfort are likely to be identified and had better be addressed as soon as possible. Third, beliefs regarding hopelessness, helplessness, and dependence, particularly those expressed in all-or-nothing terms, can also be identified for initial therapeutic intervention.

Certainly, beliefs of this nature are not unique to alcohol-troubled individuals, and a variety of other irrational ideas may well be important in any given case. Hypothetico-deductive assessment during the initial stages of the treatment can identify these irrational beliefs and provide immediate as well as persistent disputes to correct them. Left unaddressed, these issues might well impede therapeutic progress and result in the client's discontinuing treatment.

GOAL SETTING

RET encourages therapists to engage actively and directively with clients in setting realistic therapeutic goals. This aspect of treatment is particularly important in working with clients who present a large degree of resistance or denial. Often when therapeutic intervention fails to be achieved, attributions regarding the alcoholic client's lack of motivation are made by the therapist (Miller, 1985), and attributions of hopelessness are made by the client. More accurately seen, there may be a joint failure to agree upon achievable goals. A client's lack of progress may very well reflect an overt or covert decision that the goals of therapy are unnecessary, inappropriate, or unachievable. If so, agreeing on goals allows a more realistic approach to efforts to redirect the treatment undertaken.

An important area of therapeutic goal setting is the controversial "controlled drinking" issue (Marlott, 1983; W. R. Miller, 1983). It may be questioned whether a goal of moderating a given individual's alcohol use is appropriate or whether abstinence is indicated in all cases. The research as we review it suggests that choosing the goal of controlled drinking versus abstinence depends largely on the characteristics of the client under consideration.

Clearly, a large number of individuals do return to a moderate or asymptomatic level of alcohol use. On the other hand, there appears to be growing agreement that for certain individuals controlled drinking as a goal does not meet with much long-term success and therefore has little practical clinical utility. This group includes those showing a high degree of physical dependence, those who have repeatedly failed at attempts at controlled drinking, and those who are older and presumably have a longer drinking history. With younger individuals without a high degree of physical dependence, no medical complications, and relative vocational and social stability, moderation may be an appropriate goal and can be considered. It is the professional's role and expert responsibility to guide this determination.

It must be added that within the RET framework, goals can be renegotiated if data gathered during therapy support a change. Whether or not a given alcohol-troubled individual chooses to engage in moderation or abstinence as a self-control strategy, the basic procedures, philosophy, and techniques of rational-emotive therapy are applicable. The important thing is that the client is directly and repeatedly involved in setting goals. A cost-benefit analysis can be done on both issues. For example, an individual who already is showing evidence of liver impairment, who drinks on a daily basis, who has drunk for a number of years, and who has also experienced multiple job and family problems as the result of alcohol use is best directed toward the goal of abstinence. One of the most effective ways to do this is to share with the client your perception as an experienced therapist of what the research data referred to above concludes. A long-term alcoholic may be at medical risk even with small amounts of alcohol, and while it might be more comfortable and even more achievable in the short term to moderate the client's alcohol intake, the long-term beneficial results of moderation are clearly questionable.

The same cost-benefit analysis can be done with less severely involved individuals. In each case both the long-term and short-term benefits and risks of moderation are discussed. By analyzing these goal choices in the cost-benefit fashion and obtaining from the client some agreement to set initial goals in a tentative way for a specified trial period, an appropriate goal of moderation might be determined jointly. Such a goal may be specified in terms of concrete decreases in the amount consumed, in the time spent drinking, and/or in the number of drinking events in a given week. Careful and honest records would need to be kept by the client and a change in drinking pattern maintained for a substantial period of time before the goal would be considered as achieved. Clearly, this would not be something very realistic for most severe abusers. A more realistic approach might be to reestablish some conditional self-control through a period of abstinence with agreed-upon but gradual experimentation, and with a return to controlled drinking at a later time.

Why do we view specific goal setting as so important with alcohol- and drug-abusing clients? Our experience suggests that these clients have not gotten into the fix that they are in overnight. It also seems fairly safe to say that they have, on a number of occasions, attempted unsuccessfully to change or to stop their substance abuse. Their decision to change has not been followed with vigorous and sustained action, however. Goal setting can serve as a concrete commitment to follow the decision to change with actions to support it. Additionally, when clients with authority problems are involved in setting goals that are meaningful to them, oppositional resistance typical of this group may be avoided. There is some commonsense as well as research support for the notion that people are more likely to sustain effort with respect to goals that they themselves select rather than those that are imposed upon them (Bandura, 1982).

Self-efficacy is enhanced by the achievement of goals, and goal appear more likely to be achieved when the client is engaged in setting them. The literature on therapeutic change in appetitive behaviors in general further suggests that goal setting as a process, when it is explicit, improves the chances of goals toward self-regulation or the modification of difficult habits being realized (Oxford, 1985).

This is of critical importance since responsibility for self-management and enhanced self-efficacy (or, in rational-emotive terms, self-acceptance) are important therapeutic themes. Joint goal setting can be used to support the client's idea that effective self-regulation and responsible self-direction are achievable. Clearly, this will be more important with some clients than with others. Clients with high degrees of depression, helplessness, and self-damnation may well require a good deal more vivid and directive efforts to help them come to believe that they are capable of accepting responsibility for the effectiveness, first, of their treatment and, in the long run, of the management of their substance abuse as well as its emotional and behavioral complications.

A final point to make regarding goal setting: Don't try to coerce the clients to adopt your goal. In cases where the therapist's and client's goals for the client significantly diverge, you can decide whether (a) to work with the client to reduce her or his drinking, (b) to refuse to work with the client, or (c) to attempt persistently to change the client's goal. We prefer to adopt the first choice by default—not because it is desirable, but because the other two are unhelpful. The second choice reinforces not only dichotomous thinking but also rejection of the client — who then may feel hostility toward helping professionals for being rejected. The third option, we believe, is undesirable because it will result in poor rapport—because the client and therapist will be continually at cross-purposes. The first option accepts the clients and gets down to the business of changing the way clients think about drinking and what they think to make them drink.

Remember that clients' therapeutic goals are not cast in stone. They may eventually adopt the goal of abstinence when the goal of moderation has proven to be elusive. We believe it is best to propose an experiment when therapist and client goals are discrepant. Clients can be directly involved in collecting evidence to determine whether their goals are realistic. It has generally been our experience that people have more difficulty changing their addiction to alcohol while they are still drinking and therefore they had better stop completely, at least in the initial stages of therapy—but this is not necessarily agreed to by all clients. When an individual adopts a controlled drinking strategy, despite the therapist's advice to the contrary, an experiment may be undertaken to determine whether this results in specific benefits or leads to continued alcohol-related problems.

Some would argue that this is deluding the clients into thinking that the therapist is agreeing with their goal. This, of course, need not be the case. Clients can be told quite clearly that the therapist views this goal as unrealistic but that in the interest of therapy and helping them, the therapist is willing to work along with them on achieving sobriety, providing they are rigorously honest in assessing the success and relevance to the primary goal—reducing the alcohol-related problems.

We often find it useful to specify a contract in terms of concrete rules for moderate drinking as well as for record keeping. If the contract is not kept by clients, their lapse is forcefully addressed in therapy and, if need be, they can be confronted with the facts and a more appropriate goal can be undertaken. We take the view that setting rigid generalizations about the most appropriate goals for all alcohol-troubled individuals early in treatment may well result in some individuals terminating treatment early and needlessly suffering from their alcohol abuse for an unspecified period of time.

When individuals come to therapy with many indicators of severe alcohol or substance-abuse problems, the initial goal is to directly address limiting their abuse. Although there are many associated emotional, behavioral, and social difficulties that alcohol-troubled individuals experience, treating those before agreeing with the client on the goal of managing the substance abuse puts the cart before the horse.

In many cases the strategy of first addressing clients' personality and coping problems misses the obvious and can often result in unproductive treatment. As a result, addicts may become more socially skilled and less anxious, but they will probably still continue drinking pathologically. Although it can be argued that alcoholics may be better able to address their pathological drinking after learning to cope with their marital, vocational, and family problems, in our experience that is not usually the case. First, they had better learn how to reduce or eliminate their drinking.

We are often asked if we will continue to work with clients who continue to abuse their substance of choice. Some would argue that to do so is to participate in their denial of the problem. This is not necessarily the case, however, when one views recovery from substance abuse as a developmental process. By continuing to work with clients despite their "slips" or lapses in control, we can demonstrate and model both acceptance and high frustration tolerance. In the majority of our cases we have found that the most realistic approach consists of emphasizing progress rather than perfection in the setting and attainment of goals.

Chapter 5
Changing Addictive Thinking

RET with alcoholics and other addicts assumes that it is largely clients' self-defeating thoughts, and resulting feelings and actions, that sabotage their lives. One will often hear recovering alcoholics involved in Alcoholics Anonymous (AA) state that since they are not actively drinking, their problem is now their "thinking". "Thinking" rather than "drinking" is what leads individual alcoholics and other addicts either toward or away from their next drink or drug. Philosophical changes supported by various self-instructional slogans (e.g., "Easy Does it", "Live and Let Live", "One Day at a Time") are a large part of the AA program, in which thousands have been helped. This clearly recognizes the critical connection between changing patterns of automatic thoughts and more general beliefs and successful recovery from addiction. What alcoholics and other addicts tell themselves about their problem, the difficult emotions they experience in attempting to address their problem, and, most importantly, what they tell themselves about themselves for having their problem are the key beliefs that RET aims at helping clients change.

In this chapter we use the term *addictive thinking* to refer to the alcoholic or drug-abusing individual's set of beliefs, self-statements, and/or attributions about: (a) their problem with alcohol and/or other drugs, (b) the many disturbed emotions that this problem engenders and the disordered emotions produced in their attempts to change, and (c) beliefs and self-statements about themselves as people. We will first review some general considerations in disputing addictive thinking and then outline specific techniques utilized in RET for effective and varied disputation of difficult-to-change beliefs. Finally, we will provide our view of the specific content of alcoholic or addictive thinking and suggest some model counterarguments for these beliefs.

52

GENERAL CONSIDERATIONS IN DISPUTING

Addictive thinking, like other forms of irrational thinking, is often automatic, nonconscious, overlearned and continually practiced. As such, it is often resistant to change. In addition, alcoholics and other addicts are often quite unaware of the connections between their thoughts, feelings and actions. Therefore, it is best, in early stages of work with these clients, to demonstrate this connection didactically, through example, and whenever possible, through actual experience in the therapy session. Sometimes clients want to explore "why they drink". This has come from a fairly popular and widely held misunderstanding regarding psychotherapy as a search for the causes of human problems. In contrast, disputing involves a process in which the therapist assists the client to take more and more responsibility for *identifying* and *changing* self-defeating *thoughts*. Clients are most likely to progress if immediate attention is given to teaching them about this process.

Disputing is the process of challenging the irrational beliefs in a logical, empirical, philosophical, and scientific manner. In this book we often oversimplify this process by offering concrete examples of specific irrational beliefs and effective disputational statements. This does not imply, however, that the particular illustration is the best or the only way to approach a given client. Therapists prefer different styles. Learning to rely upon your own style and language as well as learning to understand the uniqueness of the client you are presently working with is crucial in persuasive disputing. Regardless of how elegant your disputing, the client may well miss the point if attention is not given to the client's language ability and cognitive style. An extreme mismatch between therapist and client rarely results in effective disputing.

We advocate a flexible and persistent approach to disputing irrational beliefs with the above considerations in mind. Some clients appear to respond best to directive, didactic, or instructional forms of disputing. Others readily appear to benefit most from homework assignments, which behaviorally assist in disputing their irrational self-statements. While some sophisticated clients may benefit from understanding the subtleties of their distorted interpretations and evaluations, others may do just as well by persistently practicing coping self-statements as antidotes to their more rigidly held irrational beliefs. The bottom line is to convey to the client in a direct and personally meaningful way that their thoughts, their feelings and their drinking or drug use behaviors are importantly connected. They are shown that they can learn to stop this destructive behavior through changing their crooked thoughts and inappropriate emotions.

Disputing is usually best done immediately and specifically; by carefully observing clients' affect in the first or second sessions, you can question them about feelings at that moment and then attempt to elicit their thoughts. This immediate experience can help demonstrate the crucial connection between and among thoughts, feelings, and actions. In addition, a whole host of common examples, stories or personal experiences can be used to illustrate these connections in a more didactic or metaphorical way. When using such personal materials or examples, you can always question clients about whether they have ever thought or felt that way. This can further help them personally identify problem thoughts and their consequences.

Many of us who are experienced in working with these clients have developed certain simple phrases that can be used self-instructionally by clients. You can encourage clients to "talk sense to yourself" about drinking or drug use. In addition, it is often useful to provide clients with some criteria for judging whether their thoughts are "sensible or not sensible," that is, are rational or irrational.

Maultsby's rules for rational thinking (Maultsby, 1979) can be adapted here. Rational thinking is: (a) based on facts, (b) helps people protect themselves from probable harm, (c) helps them achieve both short-term and long-term goals, (d) helps them prevent significant conflict with others, and (e) helps them feel the positive emotions that they want to feel.

Since some clients will have difficulty in mastering these rules, simple handouts can be provided, and/or the therapist can apply these criteria to the clients' thinking. The criticial element here is for clients to discover that they can become adept at identifying their automatic thoughts, can then test whether these thoughts are sensible and helpful, and can finally come up with alternative thoughts that are more useful. It is likely that these basic elements will need to be persistently repeated so that the clients will become convinced that they can change dysfunctional feelings and behaviors by steadily addressing their irrational thinking.

Here is a list of general considerations about the disputing process that you can consider and try early in therapeutic interaction:

1. Because disputing is central to RET, quickly establish the work of therapy as involving the identification and changing of irrational beliefs, attributions, and self-statements related to the clients' specific problems with alcohol or drugs. This helps create the expectation that

this process will continue and that the more that clients become involved in therapy the more likely they are to benefit from it.

2. In initial sessions in particular, disputation that is fairly simple, concrete and pragmatic may be most useful in demonstrating to the client the connection between their thinking and consequent emotions and behaviors. Once some forms of crooked thinking about the client's drinking have been identified, the utility of these thoughts can be questioned.

3. There are a number of disputational strategies that involve dialogue and experiential approaches. In addition, most experienced therapists have developed a particular style of interacting with their clients in order to maximize their disputing persuasiveness. Ideally, the specific strategies you use as well as your style are to be flexibly adapted to the client's presenting problems, feelings, and verbal ability.

4. In order for disputing to be optimally persuasive, involve your clients in it as soon as possible. Often this can be done by using in-session occurrences to explore specific, automatic thoughts and their relationship to their immediate emotions. This can also be done with some clients by asking them to imagine either their last or some anticipated problem-drinking episode. They can then recall their thoughts and their emotional and behavioral consequences. Generally, because their habits of thought, feeling and action are so rigid, overlearned, and resistant to change, alcohol-troubled clients can benefit most from vivid and persuasive disputation (Dryden, 1984; Ellis, 1985a).

5. Sometimes your attempts to "argue" clients out of their self-defeating thoughts will not succeed. Indeed, when you find yourself working very hard to talk such clients out of their irrationality, you may well question whether you are working too hard for the client's own good. Some individuals with alcohol- or drug-problem histories are stubborn, oppositional, or passive-aggressive in their approach to authority. Overwhelming such clients with your rationality may result in more resistance. Often, in cases such as this, it is better to go back to basics. You may review the client's goals in coming to therapy, review the negative consequences of past and future drinking, explore the advantages of reducing or eliminating drinking, focus on what they might be thinking to arouse such emotions, and finally use simple and practical disputes in a less confrontational way. Once again, being right is far less therapeutic and important than being effectively persuasive, so that in the long run, clients take on the responsibility of disputing their own self-defeating ideas.

6. Some alcohol- and drug-troubled clients expect that therapy will help them discover the causes of their problems so that they can then drink normally. If you have spent some time explaining the process and goals

of outpatient treatment with RET, this expectation can be redirected. Sometimes, it is transformed into an almost too easy and solely intellectual (or lightly held) agreement with the therapist. Take care with these clients so that more and more of the responsibility for correcting self-defeating thoughts falls to them.

DISPUTING: PROCESS AND STRATEGIES

DiGiuseppe (1986) suggests that changing clients' core irrational beliefs is a complicated process that accomplishes three main goals: The first is to create considerable cognitive dissonance for clients by mustering considerable disconfirming evidence (philosophical, logical, and empirical) for the clients' irrational beliefs; second, the therapist demonstrates that the irrational belief does not solve the clients' problems, and, in fact, is dysfunctional; third, the therapist helps the client develop a more rational belief and demonstrates that it is more helpful and has more supporting evidence than the irrational belief.

Nine disputation strategies are listed to help accomplish these goals:

1. The therapist disputes the irrational belief to show its logical fallacies.
2. The therapist attempts to assume the irrational belief is true and then explores what deductions could be made about the world if it were true and then empirically tests these deductions.
3. The therapist helps the client experience the ability of the irrational belief to explain important life events. That is, does the irrational belief include accurate attribution for events?
4. The therapist helps clients review how holding the irrational belief has helped or hurt them.
5. Steps one to four are repeated over and over again to help convince the client that the irrational belief is false or self-defeating.
6. The therapist helps the client construct a new rational belief to replace the irrational belief.
7. The therapist explores the new rational beliefs for logical fallacies.
8. The therapist makes deductions from the rational beliefs and then tests these deductions to see if the rational belief leads to more accurate predictions about the world than do the irrational beliefs.
9. The therapist helps the client predict how changing to new rational beliefs will affect their behavior and then examines whether the change in behavior will be more advantageous than the behavior that followed from the irrational belief.

however, also emphasizes getting at clients' irrational beliefs that lie behind their disturbed feelings, as well as helping them behave more efficiently in their real-life behaviors by rehearsing them for this during role-plays.

Here, for example, is the kind of role-play script that you can adapt for use with alcoholics and drug abusers:

Therapist: "Now that you're working on stopping drinking, let's help you get ready for employment. You said that you were anxious about how to interview for a job, after being unemployed for so long because of your indulgence in alcohol. Is that right?"

Client: "Yes I get so anxious at every job interview I hardly know what to say."

Therapist: "Okay. Let's role-play a typical interview, to see how you can work on your anxiety and also have a good interview. I'll play a potential employer and you be yourself as a job applicant."

Client: "Fine."

Therapist: "Mr. Jones, I understand you would like to work for us as a bookkeeper. Can you tell me something about yourself and why you think you're qualified for the job we have open?"

Client: "Yes. I — uh — I think I — uh — could do a good job. That is, I — uh —."

Therapist: "Looks like you're already nervous!"

Client: "I am. I can hardly get my words out. Guess I really want that job!"

Therapist: "Too much! What are you telling yourself right now, to make yourself so anxious?"

Client: "Uh — let me see. What am I telling myself? Yes: 'I really *need* this job. After all the drinking I've been through, I've *got* to get it – in order to redeem myself."

Therapist: "Right! That's what's making you anxious — those *needy* thoughts. But, granting that you *want* this job very much, why *must* you have it?"

Client: "Yes, I see what you mean. I don't absolutely *need* it, though it would be very good for me if I got it."

Therapist: "True. But getting this job won't *redeem* you. Why *won't* it?"

Client: "Uh — Yes! I don't have to be redeemed for my past boozing. Drinking was rotten behavior but it didn't make me a rotten person."

Therapist: "Right! I'm glad you see that now. It will be fine if you get this job. But getting it won't perfume your shithood! You *acted* shittily but were *never* a worm."

Client: "No, I wasn't. So I need no redemption. Only a good job!"

Therapist: "*Desire*, not need one."

Client: "Yes, desire one very much."

Therapist: "Good! *Now* how do you feel?"

Client: "Much less anxious."

Therapist: "I thought so. Now back to the role-playing: Mr. Jones, I understand you would like to work for us as a bookkeeper. Can you tell me something about yourself and why you think you're qualified for the job we have open?"

Client: "I—uh. Well, I studied bookkeeping in both high school and community college and I worked as a bookeeper for five years — and loved it! I really want to try it again."

Therapist: "But I see by your resume that you haven't worked for two years at anything. How about that?"

Client: "Well — uh. Well, I could lie and tell you I went back to school during that time. But you'll probably find out the truth from my last employer, anyway. So I might as well tell you it right now. Up until six months ago I was drinking like a fish. That's how I lost my last job — and everything else. But for the last six months I've been entirely off the stuff and attending at least one AA meeting every day. So now I'm really ready to go back to work. And I mean, this time, work!"

Therapist: "Good. You're doing well, so far, and you've obviously lost your nervousness. But watch your eyes! They keep looking down and not at me. And maybe you'd better add, just to back up your story, that if I, the interviewer want it, you are quite willing to let me talk with your AA sponsor and perhaps a few other AA regulars, to show that you really have been abstaining for the last six months."

Client: "That sounds like a good idea."

With continued role-playing, like that shown in the above excerpt, you can let your addicted clients reveal and express their feelings, and also reveal and dispute their irrational beliefs that lie behind disturbances the role-playing brings out, and finally rehearse some good techniques of solving their practical problems, like getting a job, relating to family members and succeeding in school.

HUMOR AS A THERAPEUTIC METHOD

RET especially favors the use of humor to help reduce alcoholics' and drug abusers' irrational beliefs to absurdity and to help addicts give them up. This is because rational-emotive therapy sees people's disturbances as largely resulting from their taking certain ideas too seriously, sacredizing them, and almost completely losing one's sense of humor about how to get along in life (Ellis, 1977a, 1977b, 1987).

Humor is often a fine antidote against disturbance and compulsion because it has a powerful emotive as well as cognitive element.

Laughter can dramatically jolt your clients out of their self-defeating habits and cleverly push them into anti-addictive action. Like stories, poems and parables, humor also has an analogical and metaphorical element that goes beyond common digital thinking and therefore has a pronounced emotive way of combating disturbance.

RET has pioneered in using rational humorous songs with seriously addicted (and other) clients. These songs are often given as homework assignments for alcohol and substance abusers to sing several times to themselves when their anxiety, their depression, and/or their low frustration tolerance is supposedly driving them to abuse or encouraging them to remain addicted (Ellis, 1977a, 1977b, 1987). Some of the rational humorous songs that have been found to be effective include these:

Drinking, I'm Always Thinking of You
(Tune: "Margie" by Con Conrad and J. Russell Robinson)

Drinking. I'm always thinking of you!
Drinking, I'll tell the world I love you!
Don't forget your promise to me —
I can drink and never sink beyond the brink!
Oh, drinking, with you to sweetly guide me, I am never blue!
After all is said and done,
There is really only one —
Oh, stinking drinking, it's you!
    (Lyrics by Albert Ellis, Copyright 1980 by Institute for Rational-Emotive Therapy)

Beautiful Hangup
(Tune: "Beautiful Dreamer" by Stephen Foster)

Beautiful hangup, why should we part
When we have shared our whole lives from the start
We are so used to taking one course,
Oh, what a crime it would be to divorce!
Beautiful hangup, don't go away!
Who will befriend me if you do not stay?
Though you still make me look like a jerk,
Living without you would take too much work!
    — Living without you would take too much work!
    (Lyrics by Albert Ellis, Copyright 1980 by Institute for Rational-Emotive Therapy)

I'm Just Wild About Drinking
(Tune: "I'm Just Wild About Harry" by Eubie Blake)

Oh, I'm just wild about drinking
And drinking's wild about me!
When I am drinking I just keep blinking
At dangers that threaten me!
Oh, I'm just wild about drinking
And stinking thinking I buy!
If I want follies to stack up,
With booze I'll shack up
And never back up
Until I crack up and die!
   (Lyrics by Albert Ellis, Copyright 1987 by Institute for Rational-Emotive
Therapy)

I Wish I Were Not Crazy
(Tune: "Dixie" by Dan Emmett)

Oh, I wish I were really put together—
Smooth and fine as patent leather!
Oh, how great to be rated innately sedate!
But I'm afraid that I was fated
To be rather aberrated—
Oh, how sad to be mad as my Mom and my Dad!
Oh, I wish I were not crazy! Hooray, hooray!
I wish my mind were less inclined
To be the kind that's hazy!
I could agree to really be less crazy
But I, alas, am just too goddamed lazy!
   (Lyrics by Albert Ellis, Copyright 1977 by Institute for Rational-Emotive
Therapy)

Chapter 8
Specific RET Behavioral Techniques for Use with Addicts

As noted previously, general or unspecialized RET is virtually synonymous with cognitive-behavioral therapy (CBT) and therefore can and does use many of the commonly employed behavioral methods that often work with alcoholics and drug abusers (Bellack & Hersen, 1985, Ellis, 1985a; Ellis & Bernard, 1983, 1985; Ellis & Dryden, 1987).

Preferential or specialized RET particularly uses, in fact very frequently uses, the following behavioral methods that have not only been shown to help addicts stop their overindulgence but that also seem to be effective with helping them to reduce their irrational thinking and their accompanying emotional disturbances. Here are some of the main behavioral methods that you, as a practitioner of RET, can often employ with substance abusers.

IN VIVO DESENSITIZATION

Behavior therapy and cognitive-behavior therapy frequently use Wolpe's (1982) method of systematic densensitization, which is largely imaginary and which relies on relaxation techniques. Preferential RET, on the other hand, tends to favor in vivo desensitization for alcoholics and drug abusers, as well as for many other kinds of clients (Ellis, 1962, 1973a, 1979b, 1985a; Ellis & Becker, 1982; Ellis & Harper, 1975). However, although RET favors encouraging phobics to risk going into the elevators or onto the escalators of which they are irrationally afraid, it does not encourage addicts who are (realistically) afraid of drinking or drugging to go into bars or to stay with their substance-user friends. On the contrary, it advises them to avoid this kind of risk taking, because it is likely to lead to a return to abusing.

At the same time, when addicts have stopped drinking and taking drugs and are ready to work on their original anxiety that helped drive them to addiction, RET frequently uses in vivo desensitization to encourage them to overcome their anxieties and phobias. Thus, you can encourage clients with job-seeking or public-speaking anxiety to actually take the risks of looking for jobs and speaking in public until they see that they can do these things and lose their anxiety about doing them. In using in vivo desensitization with alcoholics and drug abusers, remember that they are often more vulnerable and more easily impelled to intoxication than are many other clients. So treat them more gently and less implosively than you would treat some of your nonabusers.

IMPLOSIVE DESENSITIZATION

For many regular clients, RET favors implosive in vivo desensitization — for example, encouraging clients with elevator phobias to get on 20 or more elevators a day so that they can quickly and efficiently fight their irrational fears. As we noted in the previous section pertaining to in vivo desensitization, this technique, especially when used implosively, may be too rough for vulnerable alcoholics and drug abusers and is therefore to be used with caution or else to be avoided. However, for those clients who want to try it and who have already given up their addiction for a safe period of time, you can sometimes use implosive in vivo desensitization.

In one of our cases, for example, was an alcoholic woman who had refrained from drinking for a year but who was still exceptionally anxious about speaking up in class. She was given the assignment of raising her hand to ask a question or make a comment several times during every psychology class she took. When she forced herself, in spite of her anxiety, to do this, she completely overcame her phobia within six weeks and then voluntarily went on to implosively work against, and soon to give up, her fear of going dancing and of socializing at dances and other affairs.

REINFORCEMENT AND PENALIZING

RET, being behavioral as well as cognitive and emotive, frequently uses reinforcement and operant-conditioning methods to help people to stop abusing substances and to stay stopped (Bernard, 1986; Ellis, 1969b, 1985a; Ellis & Bernard, 1984, 1986). It has addicts contract with themselves and their therapist to only permit themselves to do something enjoyable, such as take a pleasant vacation or socialize, *after* they have stopped their addiction.

This often helps addicts, but not as much as reinforcement tends to help nonaddicts. Because many addicts receive so much immediate pleasure and temporary surcease from anxiety when they imbibe alcohol or drugs (especially drugs like cocaine and heroin), they are frequently unwilling to substitute another pleasure for the enormous gratification they are sure they will get when they imbibe. So many of the usual reinforcements will just not work.

Nonetheless, you can try contracting with some of your alcoholics to only allow themselves to go on vacations, to read, to listen to music, or to do other things they greatly enjoy *after* they have stopped drinking. Sometimes this kind of reinforcement will work, and if it doesn't you can use various other RET techniques outlined in this book.

One of the best of these other methods, and one that we often try with our difficult customers (DCs), if and when they will accept them, are stiff penalties when they imbibe or take addictive substances. Here, alcoholics can agree to pay 500 dollars, to do 100 push-ups, or to reward someone or some cause they detest each time they take a single drink. Do not trust alcoholics to carry out these penalties for drinking, since they can easily fail to enact them and then lie and say that they did. See that they are closely monitored (by a close friend, family member, or yourself), so that they actually carry out the agreed-upon penalties and do so very shortly after they have had each drink.

You can also effectively use penalties with addicts to help them overcome their other problems. Thus, when they are no longer drinking or drugging, they can burn a large amount of money every time they refuse to look for a job, to socialize, or to study for an important course. They can thereby use appropriate penalties to work against their ego anxiety and their discomfort anxiety and to employ them to combat various kinds of avoidances and dysfunctional behaviors, especially those that contribute significantly to their addictions. They can also combat their self-deprecation about their alcoholism and substance abuse (and about anything else) by reinforcing themselves with something pleasurable after they cut down their self-castigation and by penalizing themselves severely every time they indulge in self-downing.

RESPONSE PREVENTION

A number of behavior therapists have found that in serious compulsions and addictions one of the most effective techniques is response prevention — that is, monitoring and controlling addicts for a period of time, so that they find it almost impossible to indulge in their addiction (Marlatt & Gordon, 1985; Williamson, 1985). RET heartily endorses this method, especially when other techniques of inducing addicts to stop and stay stopped are ineffective (Ellis, 1981, 1985a).

To use response prevention you can induce the alcoholic or drug abuser to agree to be temporarily institutionalized and supervised in a setting that makes their use of addictive chemical substances impossible. Or even in their own home setting they can be monitored around the clock for several days or weeks by relatives or friends who literally stop them from imbibing alcohol or drugs. Once subjected to this kind of response prevention for a while, they may then be able to stay stopped by monitoring themselves.

RELAPSE PREVENTION

Mark Twain's famous remark about smoking can also be applied to drinking and modified as follows: "It's easy to stop drinking. I've done it a hundred times!" Relapse prevention, therefore, is an important part of the RET anti-alcoholism and anti-drug-abusing progam (Ellis, 1982a, 1982b; Velten, 1986).

RET-oriented relapse prevention is cognitive, emotive, and behavioral. Cognitiveiy, you teach addicts to be prepared, in advance, for possible setbacks, to look for Irrational Beliefs, (e.g., "I can get away with experimenting with a small amount of drinking"), and to actively and persistently keep disputing these IBs. Emotively, you can push your clients to forcefully use rational coping statements (e.g., "I can *easily* fall back to boozing again if I am not *constantly* on guard").

Behaviorally, you can encourage your clients to use several techniques, such as:

Stimulus Control. Rigorously stay away from addictive friends and associates, from bars and drug pushers, and from other tempting people and places.

Reinforcements. Only allow certain pleasures contingent upon the addicts' refraining from relapsing.

Penalties. Enact stiff penalties every time any relapse occurs.

Substitutions. Devise and use harmless enjoyments that are good substitutes for relapsing.

Physical distractions. Use relaxation, breathing, jogging, and other physical activities that distract from the urge to drink or to take drugs — and that also may divert one from ego anxiety, discomfort anxiety, and from self-demeaning about drinking.

Medication. If advisable, temporarily take under medical supervision antianxiety or antidepressant medication that will help allieviate the urge to relapse.

SKILL TRAINING AND PROBLEM SOLVING

Since its earliest days RET has specialized in skill training and especially social skills training (Ellis, 1956, 1957a, 1962, 1963a, 1963b, 1976a, 1978, 1979b). This is because it not only works comprehensively to change people's irrational beliefs (IBs) and dysfunctional consequences (Cs), but it also goes back to their unfortunate situations and Activating Events (As) and tries to help them change these too.

To this end, you can often help teach your addictive clients, when they could use it, communication, assertion, parental, social skills and other training. You can also help them solve practical problems, such as how to get and keep a job, how to select a good career, and how to decide which school to attend. The more successful you can help addicts to be in their everyday life problems, the less strained their lives will likely be and the less prone they may well be to alcohol and drug abuse.

Chapter 9

The Process of RET with Alcoholics and Substance Abusers

As professional psychologists who have worked with large numbers of alcoholics, we do not naively think that disputing the clients' irrational thinking (and related behavioral and emotive techniques) in therapy sessions *alone* will be effective in helping these clients make major life changes. We know that individuals troubled with problems of alcohol develop these difficulties over the course of many years. In the process of developing these problems, a host of other difficulties evolve, and, in fact, some preexisting tendencies toward self-defeating thoughts, feelings and actions are exacerbated. While we generally view clients' successful modification of maladaptive alcohol use as a prerequisite for other therapeutic progress and find that changing some of the self-talk and underlying assumptions that leads to this abuse is crucial, other issues and problems often impinge upon treatment and affect its course.

These issues may involve vocational problems, medical difficulties, or family difficulties. Other issues are the clients' participation in self-help groups and the management of underlying psychological or psychiatric problems, which can complicate the recovery from alcohol abuse. In understanding and addressing all these related treatment management issues, we find the rational-emotive perspective on human disturbance quite applicable.

STAGES OF TREATMENT

In order to address diverse treatment-management issues in RET with alcoholic and other substance-abusing clients, it would be helpful to have an overview of the treatment process that is typically encountered. For descriptive purposes, treatment can be conceptualized in phases or stages. Certainly not every case will progress from phase to phase in the same way or at the same rate, but it is within the context of this process that the various cognitive, emotive, and behavioral techniques discussed in previous chapters are applied. This is also the context in which the various case and treatment issues discussed in this chapter come up and require our attention. With this process overview in mind, Table 9.1 presents a summary of what we see as the major phases of RET with alcoholic and substance-abusing clients, as well as the most prominent focus or goals of each phase and the major cognitive and behavioral strategies likely to be associated with each.

The initial stage of therapy involves developing a therapeutic alliance, assessing and defining the nature of the problem, and jointly setting initial goals for treatment. The second state involves implementing cognitive and behavioral strategies to assist clients in specifically altering their maladaptive reliance on alcohol. The strategies used will vary for different clients, based on their particular characteristics. However, all clients will be urged to practice more control over their drinking through stimulus control techniques, behavioral contracting, and through disputing the irrational ideas that support their addiction. The third stage involves the monitoring of progress and the reassessment of goals. This stage includes a more developmental perspective of the individual client's recovery and addresses a wide variety of emotional and behavioral problems while continuing to provide support for maintaining the clients' progress in avoiding alcohol abuse. When some stability about drinking has been achieved, more effort is directed toward disputing the irrational beliefs leading to more general, self-defeating, emotional, and behavioral consequences. As therapy progresses into the final stage or phase, much of it will focus on the individual's problems with self-acceptance and work toward promoting a more rational and "addiction-proof" philosophy of living. A variety of practical and emotional adjustment problems might be discussed in this context.

TREATMENT MANAGEMENT

A practical treatment-management issue that often comes up in working with addicts is the issue of relapse. Longitudinal research suggests that alcoholic (and, we may infer, other addicts) during the full course of their problems with alcohol will experience many relapses. It seems that these setbacks are the rule rather than the exception. Despite this, in some more traditional treatment approaches, relapses are rarely discussed for fear that they may encourage or give permission to the

Table 9.1.
A Process View of RET with Alcoholics and Substance Abusers

Phase	Major Focus/Goal	Probable Cognitive Issues/Strategies	Probable Behavioral Issues/Strategies
I Initiating treatment	Establishing a noncondemning relationship; collaborating on defining the problem and setting goals; and teaching client to use treatment.	Assessment of clients' views of discomfort, of alcohol and drug effects and of themselves for having the problem to begin with; correcting clients' incorrect or irrational beliefs about treatment, their problems with alcohol, and the process of recovery.	Accurate assessment of the frequency, amplitude and duration of dysfunctional alcohol and/or substance abuse; direct instruction on the limit of therapy and how to use it to change behavior; beginning with honest definition of the problem.
II Stopping	Conditional acceptance that there is a problem and action toward the initial steps required to inhibit abuse (i.e., a decision to change and action to implement this decision).	Disrupting discomfort anxiety and helplessness. Establishing realistic expectations about time and effort required for change; while change is difficult, it isn't too hard to accomplish, and while stopping will make one uncomfortable it is tolerable.	Establishing incompatible alternatives to alcohol or substances abuse; establishing self-reinforcement strategies for not using and/or penalties for use; keeping behavioral records.
III Staying stopped	Emotional and behavioral self-management to avoid the triggers for dysfunctional use.	Didactic and dialoging teaching of the ABC-D of RET; disputing shoulds for self, others, and the world; disputing dichotomous reasoning, exaggeration of frustration and self-damnation for imperfections; basic rational-emotive problem-solving skills.	Teaching behavioral stress management (e.g., relaxation training, self-hypnosis); assertive training and behavioral rehearsal for saying no to use; social skills training and/or social problem-solving training and rehearsal.
IV Changing personal philosophy	Developing a more rational philosophy self-acceptance and a more stress-resistant life style.	Didactic and dialogic teaching of philosophy of self acceptance and tolerance for human imperfections, disputing self-rating while encouraging a rational appraisal of the consequences of decisions to think, feel, and act in a given way toward self and others.	Instruction, encouragement and direct reinforcement of expanded experiences for personal pleasure and vocational accomplishment.

client to go out and do some research on whether or not they can drink. We tend to view relapses simply as events that can have a tremendous educational value for the client. They need not be viewed as failures.

A relapse can be discussed with the client in realistic terms; namely, although relapses are certainly not to be encouraged, they are not the end of the world. A relapse does not prove conclusively that therapy has failed, nor does it prove that the client is a failure in his or her efforts at improved self-management. Rather, the most rational explanation of relapse is that some of the changes undertaken are not yet complete. In addition, as a therapist, you can show that a relapse is a product of choice even if the choice is not always conscious or apparent. Rarely does a relapse result from some uncontrollable urge to drink, despite the fact that the client might view it that way. Often, stress or specific disturbed emotions directly or indirectly precipitate a relapse. Therefore, important information for both the client and the therapist can be obtained from an honest appraisal of a relapse experience. Consequently, you quite openly discuss the possibility of relapse and how that might be handled without being overtly or covertly construed as encouraging relapse to occur.

As noted in Chapter 5, a related phenomenon is the abstinence violation effect (Marlatt & Gordon, 1985). This is a frequently experienced phenomenon when clients slip and then catastrophize about the meaning of this slip and see it as a complete loss of control and a major insult to self-esteem or self-efficacy. You can be fairly direct in discussing this in a didactic way early in treatment. You can explain that individuals who mistakenly break their contract with themselves and choose to abuse alcohol when they aim for moderation or abstinence walk a thin line between being blithely unconcerned about their mistake and damning themselves for it. Clients can be strongly encouraged to discuss their "slips" with you in order to learn from them. They can also be urged to talk sense to themselves about the meaning of a slip, in order to avoid an astinence-violation effect. We have found that as a result of this effect, therapy is often terminated when clients feel that they have so completely failed that they cannot face the therapist, or that the therapy has so completely failed them that they are indeed hopeless and have no choice but to return to their self-destructive pattern of drinking.

An additional treatment-management issue to address is homework between therapy sessions. This is a very important part of RET. Directly discuss with and lead clients to develop a positive expectation that they will make more progress if they do some work in between sessions. Based on their level of functioning and potential commitment to therapy, you can begin giving quite simple assignments, such as reading a pamphlet or listening to a tape, and then expand into more specific and detailed assignments as therapy progresses.

It is important to check up on any homework that is assigned. This tells clients that this is an important part of therapy and also provides the therapist with valuable information about their clients' involvement in the therapeutic process as well as their clients' mastery of some of the basic skills that have been encouraged in treatment. Elaborate, detailed, and highly cognitive types of homework assignments are probably not very useful for the most severe alcohol and drug abusers, particularly early in treatment. They may not be able to comprehend them and could be overwhelmed. Try to make an ongoing judgment about each individual client's capacity and willingness to undertake between-session assignments so as to make assignments realistic, practical, and achievable.

A very important treatment-management issue arises when out-patient treatment appears to be unsuccessful. This may happen only after a few sessions or may occur after a period of reasonable success in moderating drinking. At this point, you may wisely consider whether some more restrictive and/or intensive form of treatment might have a better chance of success. This can involve placement in a residential rehabilitation program, participation in a day or evening program, and/or short-term hospitalization for detoxification and more in-depth assessment.

The outcome literature does not clearly indicate that intensive and multidimensional rehabilitation programs are necessarily more effective than are more minimal forms of intervention (Miller, 1985). But for some individuals, particularly those who are having a difficult time remaining in their own community and staying drug and/or alcohol free, other options are to be carefully considered. By all means investigate the residential and day-treatment resources in your community and develop at least an informal profile of the kinds of clients with whom they appear to be most successful. When clients are faltering in their progress, but want to continue with outpatient treatment, the possibility of residential placement can still be considered as an element in the treatment contract. Clients can agree that if they don't stop imbibing, they will *then* go to a residential program, and this contract may give them the incentive to stay sober.

There is much to be said for the fact that residential rehabilitation programs in some ways provide an "easier" but not easy way for active alcoholic and/or substance-abusing clients to proceed in treatment. During their stay in such a facility they are protected from day-to-day temptations to drink and also are temporarily relieved of many of their family and vocational responsibilities as well. When they leave the facility, however, they had better develop new ways of thinking, feeling, and acting in their natural environment. *Outpatient aftercare treatment is almost always indicated.*

Give serious consideration to how you will relate to other individuals involved with the primary client who is alcoholic. Because of the nature of this addiction and the way in which it affects a number of other people — including family members, employers, community agencies and the legal system — a whole host of outsiders might have an interest in the addict's progress. A practical and commonsense approach to dealing with this issue includes addressing the concerns of significant others without violating the client's right to confidentiality and the expectation that the relationship with the therapist will be private and, to some extent, exclusive. It is best to deal early in treatment with exactly what kind of information and under what circumstances significant others will be given such information. While one client may be pleased to have a spouse involved meaningfully in treatment or might wish that the therapist provide some positive feedback and progress report to an employer, another client might resent it.

Try to be guided by a joint consensus with clients about what is in their best interest. Frequently, it will be in the best long-term interest of the client for some form of involvement of significant others to take place. With the evolution of new treatment arrangements, such as those included in employee assistance programs or mandatory treatment programs in the legal system, some clients may have relatively little choice about the therapist's involvement with third parties. Regardless, there is considerable latitude about what you can say, and this can be a productive area of discussion between you and your client. Sorting out the long-term best interest of the client and proceeding in a reasonable and moderate way toward that end is the best approach.

DISCONTINUING TREATMENT

When is it appropriate to discontinue treatment? Ideally, the decision to discontinue treatment is a joint one arrived at by you and your client. When treatment evolves according to plan, a relatively intensive phase of treatment aimed at helping clients learn to discontinue maladaptive alcohol or drug use and to maintain this change is followed by the selection of new therapeutic goals oriented toward helping clients learn to change their self-talk and irrational underlying assumptions that lead to emotional-behavioral malfunctioning. As this phase evolves, treatment can be less frequently scheduled or arranged on an as-needed basis. Clients can be encouraged to choose what they would like to work on and a variety of practical and emotional problem-solving techniques within the framework of RET can be utilized. At this point, when clients have stopped alcohol abuse and maintained this change for a reasonable period of time, possibly nine months or more, the orientation of treatment can shift to personal growth in rational self-management and to activities that enhance self-acceptance. In this more or less ideal scenario, the decision to discontinue treatment is often one in which no discrete event marks the shift in emphasis from regular treatment to as-needed contact. Discontinuing treatment follows naturally and logically from the developmental process that has taken place throughout treatment.

In the real world, decisions to discontinue treatment and/or refer to other resources occur for all varieties of reasons. Issues related to discontinuing treatment include some of the following circumstances. Sometimes a client will overtly or covertly discontinue treatment on their own accord for reasons that are unspecified. In other cases, treatment will be discontinued due to the influence of some practical problems or because a client chooses to seek some other form of treatment or self-help. In another scenario, treatment may be discontinued because it is not meeting with significant success, and more intensive resources are deemed to be appropriate. Again, treatment may be discontinued in a less than ideal way by the client's simply dropping out.

When clients decide to discontinue after a series of initial sessions and after establishing some conditional change in maladaptive alcohol use as well as mastering some rational self-management skills, they may decide that treatment has been successful enough and choose to end it. If so, try to review concretely and explicitly the client's thinking about stopping therapy. Without questioning the judgment regarding progress, describe a list of goals that might yet remain to be accomplished. Being aware of the client's past treatment history as well as their own futile efforts to change their alcohol abuse, you may well question whether their stopping treatment is premature. If this is the case, bring it up in a forthright manner.

Always give the discontinuing client the option to reinitiate treatment at the first sign of any renewed difficulties. It is helpful to review with clients some signs that suggest they return to treatment. Should you feel that discontinuing active treatment is premature, try to get the client to agree to a follow-up meeting, telephone contact, or some other specific activity at an agreed-upon future date. Show clients you have faith in their self-reliance, but also show them that having future difficulties does not constitute a failure. You can sometimes frame this by noting that alcoholism cannot be "cured," only managed. While making reasonable efforts to discuss realistically client's decision to discontinue, it is appropriate to approach differences of opinion respectfully.

Occasionally clients will discontinue treatment because they feel that treatment is ineffective, unnecessary or contrary to the principles of some self-help group in which they are involved. Once again, fully discuss this decision. Therapy may certainly create some discomfort, but clients will be more likely to discontinue because of this discomfort if initial treatment has not met with success on their terms. If you take care to create reasonable expectations and if at the outset of therapy you state that it is hard work with no guarantee of a miracle cure, the clients are more likely to remain. Further, when appropriate, you can point out that RET is consistent with involvement in self-help groups, such as Alcoholics Anonymous. If you take care to create reasonable expectations and have ongoing discussions of clients' involvement in these groups, their participation can be nicely integrated with RET.

Clients often drop out of treatment when their goals have not been met. Admittedly, some of their goals may be quite irrational or unreasonable — such as being able to continue to drink without negative consequences or finding an easy miracle cure to the multiple problems related to alcoholism. Clients also drop out for reasons that are quite personal, such as discontent with the therapist's personality or advice from significant people that therapy is unnecessary or harmful. Try to discover why people drop out, because you may get useful information for work with similar clients in the future.

While certainly not true in all cases, a number of clients drop out of treatment because they have relapsed. Follow-up in these cases can be helpful in changing their misconceptions about the meaning of relapse and may dispose them to seeking further help. While we have no hard statistics on the number of alcoholic clients that relapse, we think that this number can be minimized by the goal setting and immediate and directive nature of RET as well as by the effort to create realistic goals and expectations.

Another issue arises when treatment is discontinued after clients have refused referral to another resource and the client's condition has followed a deteriorating course despite outpatient intervention. If this occurs, you had better objectively and realistically try to determine whether or not the method and setting you provided is intensive enough to address clients' problems effectively. As stated in a previous section, when clients deteriorate, suffer multiple relapses, and have increasing vocational and family complications, referral to another more intensive treatment resource is often indicated. Most often, referral for some form of inpatient treatment can be considered. While it may be theoretically possible for clients to persevere and benefit from

E-RET—H

out-patient treatment, practical complications may make this persistence unlikely. You can then prudently consider whether persisting in outpatient treatment does not prevent your clients and/or concerned other parties from seeking more *effective* forms of intervention.

Continuing in outpatient treatment despite a deteriorating course may create the misconception that effective help is being provided when it is not or that no effective help is possible when it is. Because cases where outpatient treatment is not sufficient are common, it is clearly important to set specific goals and monitor progress on a regular basis, particularly with clients presenting severe forms of alcoholism and other substance-use disorders.

Consider the following general principles in determining when and how to discontinue treatment for a particular client. Where goals have been agreed upon, then discontinuation can follow you and your client's joint determination of satisfactory attainment of many or at least some of these goals. Discontinuing treatment after effective initial efforts, when clients strongly wish to discontinue and "go it alone," can be agreed upon with the client being encouraged to make some follow-up efforts. When clients decide to discontinue treatment because goals are not being attained or because they feel therapy is in some way incompatible with other methods of self-help, try to institute concrete ways of discussing this decision. In all events, clients' decisions to discontinue treatment are ultimately theirs.

SUMMARY

Treatment-process issues are often quite important in the treatment management of alcoholic and other substance-abusing clients. This is particularly true with clients with the more severe forms of the disorder, since they are likely to have multiple complicating difficulties. These problems do not develop overnight, so effective treatment may be a long-term affair.

In order to help the clients change the thoughts, feelings, and behaviors that constitute these disorders, it is useful to orient clients toward achieving progress rather than perfection. Persistence through-out several phases of the treatment process is required. In the initial phase, emphasis can be upon establishing a persuasive therapeutic relationship, setting achievable goals, and beginning the process of teaching clients how to dispute their dysfunctional thoughts, which keep them upset and drinking or abusing. In later phases of treatment, particularly after the client has established some conditional control over addictive behavior, emphasis can shift to rational-emotive self-management of the cognitive, emotional, behavioral, and situational triggers for substance abuse. Final stages of treatment will involve emotional and practical problem solving to assist clients in staying stopped as well as in reorganizing their lives and altering the underlying irrational beliefs that were major contributors to the problem in the first place.

A developmental perspective on the treatment of alcoholism suggests treatment planning through joint involvement with the client in goal setting and assessment. Case-management issues and complications, particularly with more severe cases, are to be anticipated. It would be unwise for the therapist to think that psychotherapy in and of itself will result in clients' full recovery. While RET can make a major contribution to this end, it is probably not the only thing that a client will need to do or commit themselves to in order to change and maintain this change in their everyday lives. A prudent therapist will encourage clients to explore all sorts of other resources for modifying and maintaining changes in their previously maladaptive life-style.

When goals have been met throughout the various phases of treatment, consideration should be given to discontinuing or changing the treatment process. In severe cases, referral to other resources for more intensive or more specialized treatment ought to be considered. While drop-outs from treatment are not at all uncommon, these can be minimized by a goal-oriented approach, realistic expectations, the use of the most effective and efficient methods available, prudent consideration of the many other complicating problems clients present, and periodic reviews of progress.

Chapter 10
Working with the Enabler

Alcoholics and drug abusers almost always have families — wives, husbands, mother, father, son, daughter — and the addiction touches all of their lives. They have to live the pain and suffering of seeing their loved one destroyed by the addiction, and they have to live with the disruption to family life that comes with substance abuse. Anyone familiar with substance abusers knows how hurtful and cruel they can be to their loved ones and how the addict or alcoholic can sap family resources. Family members live in continued fear of fallout from drunkenness—anger, verbal abuse, physical abuse, or destruction of property (Brown, 1985; Royce, 1981). In recognition of the effect of addiction on the family, AA has for years approved self-help groups for spouses (Al-Anon) and for children (Al-Ateen) of alcoholics. This section will deal with the spouses who live with the substance abuser.

Much of the literature on alcoholism and drug abuse refers to substance abuse as a family disease (Paolino & McGrady, 1975; Ward & Faillace, 1970; Brown, 1985). Sometimes spouses are referred to as *codependents* and the term *enabler* is frequently used to describe a spouse, parent, child or friend who encourages the substance abuser in subtle and usually unconscious ways. We believe that discussion of these terms often contain the *nominal fallacy*. Because the problem has been recognized and named, an assumption is made that it has been explained. While we do believe some people are enablers of substance abusers, and some family members are so dependent on being with a substance abuser that they appear addicted and therefore codependent, little has been written or researched to help understand, explain, and change the behavior of these individuals. We shall try to present a rational-emotive theory of enablers and suggest ways of helping enablers step out of that role.

TYPES OF ENABLERS

Enablers are individuals who appear to help the alcoholic and substance abuser continue in their addiction. There are several ways that enablers can facilitate addiction. The first is by providing the addict with alcohol, drugs, or the money to secure them, or by joining them in the use and and abuse of the drugs. This type openly supports the persons' habit. We call this type of enabler, the "joiner".

A second type of enabler clearly states they are opposed to their loved one's drinking or drug use and makes an open campaign to try and change him or her. We call this type the "messiah". In their attempt to help, the messiah usually intervenes for the addict or alcoholic in such a way that prevents them from receiving the natural consequences of their drunkenness and loss of control. They "understand" the problem and want to help make things better. So they *rescue* the alcoholic or drug addict from the negative consequences of substance abuse. If the abuser uses all of her or his money on drugs, or is broke, or is fired because of being high, the messiah will make a loan or gift of money or pay the bills. If the alcoholic or drug addict becomes verbally abusive and insulting, the messiah will stand the pain because he or she knows "it is the alcohol speaking" and will save the relationship because the abuser "needs" them. The net effect of the messiah's behavior is to insulate or cushion the loved one from the effects of the addiction. This prevents the alcoholic or addict from even experiencing the full impact of the natural punishment or consequences of substance abuse. This has the undesired effect of keeping the addiction going.

A third type of enabler is the "silent sufferer". Silent sufferers do not make an attempt to change the substance abuser, nor do they make rescue attempts to help the alcoholic or drug addict with problems caused by the substance abuse. Rather, silent sufferers are always there. They will not confront the drunk with their obvious abuse, nor will they mention the bills that can't be paid, the friends who have been insulted, or the insults they have received. They just take it. They absorb the pain and are there for the abuser. The silent sufferer also prevents the alcoholic and drug addict from experiencing the natural consequences and punishments of substance abuse by always being there and pretending that nothing is wrong. The silent sufferer's pretending makes it easy for the alcoholic and drug addict to deny that there are problems resulting from their drinking or drug use. The silent sufferer colludes in a conspiracy to deny the problem and to present an image to the world that all is well. Silent sufferers have a great tolerance for pain and a great ability to act and deny.

DETECTING AN ENABLER

Each of us has had the experience of treating someone in therapy for a long period of time before we discovered that the client was involved with an alcoholic or drug-abusing family member or lover. We have been surprised at our own inability to have detected the problem. We were more surprised at the client's unwillingness or inability to notice or mention that a significant other was an alcoholic or drug addict and that the client was unwilling or unable to share the abuse suffered from the alcoholic or drug-abusing significant other. These cases have usually involved the following problems: cases of spouse abuse; cases of child abuse and neglect; cases of females with serious depression; families where people do not talk to each other for months or years; cases with serious family financial problems despite what appears to be adequate income; cases of child behavior problems where one parent refuses to be involved with the treatment — usually the uninvolved parent turns out to be the alcoholic; cases with a young adult child who does not work; and finally, cases of serious marital dysfunction where one spouse refuses to come for marital therapy.

Not all families who present with these problems have an alcoholic or drug-abusing member hidden in the closet. Nor do we believe that the average clinician should expect alcohol or drug abuse in all people they treat. However, we do recognize that many well-trained clinicians miss problems of substance abuse in a family, and the net effect of treatment without this knowledge has helped the enabler be a better enabler. In such cases, the treatment may have had the unintended result of the client's developing greater tolerance for suffering. Given that so many enablers do not recognize that they play this role, and given that some enablers—such as joiners and silent sufferers—accept the drinking or drug abuse of their significant other as unchangeable and the normal state of affairs—how do clinicians spot these problems? One solution is to ask all clients that you see detailed questions to uncover substance abuse or an enabling pattern. We reject this as too inefficient.

Another strategy is to question the patients who do show the problems mentioned above. Another strategy is to follow up *any* mention of alcohol or drug use mentioned by a client with specific questions covering who was using drugs and alcohol, how much was consumed, and how frequently the consumption occurs? Frequently, enablers are too embarrassed to admit that a problem exists and they will just mention that they fought with their spouse often at parties where the spouse drank too much. Questions concerning the frequency and degree of drug and alcohol use and how frequently the family conflict occurs around drugs and alcohol can bring out a torrent of information.

Another strategy is to be aware of patterns of interpersonal relationships that enablers usually display and then pursue questions about the drug and alcohol use of significant others when you see clients who display those patterns of interpersonal behavior.

For example, clinical folklore maintains that children of alcoholics frequently marry alcoholics. Thus enablers are likely to have the same traits ascribed to adult children of alcoholics (Brown, 1985). These traits are purported to be (a) a demand to control others and their environment totally, and (b) a fear of assertion coupled with the extreme demand for love and approval, which shows itself by repeated efforts to please others.

Clients who present with either of these behavior patterns could be involved with alcoholic or drug-abusing significant others. Based on this hypothesis, the clinician could ask questions concerning drug or alcohol use by the significant other.

WHY HELP THE ENABLER?

One could argue that it is very difficult if not impossible to help an alcoholic or drug addict as long as one or more family members enable the patient to continue addiction. Does the successful treatment of a drug abuser or alcoholic require that the family be brought into therapy, taught about their enabling, and taught how to stop? Could working on the enabler be the first strategy to getting the primary identified patient — the alcoholic or drug addict — back on the road to sobriety? Treatment of the enabler to stop enabling could be seen as a tool for treating the addiction.

Although this direction is very tempting, we suggest that it is wrong for two reasons. First, enablers are human beings in their own right and deserve to be helped to lead healthy and satisfying lives, *regardless* of their relationship to the addict. Using them as a tool to treat the addict or alcoholic may infringe on this right. It is more important for the enabler to know several things: (a) how their philosophies of life got them into this unrewarding role; (b) if they play a similar role with other people in their life; and (c) how they can develop new philosophies of life that can lead to more satisfying interpersonal relationships. Because enablers help the addict or alcoholic to stay addicted, it is easy for them (and sometimes for therapists) to conclude erroneously that the enabler is *responsible* for changing the alcoholic or addict. Because the enabler helps the addict to maintain the addiction does not mean that the enabler *causes* the addiction. Because changing an enabler's behavior toward the addict is frequently helpful in changing the addicts, it does not follow that changing the enabler will automatically, necessarily, or even easily change the alcoholic or drug abuser. The enabler is *not* responsible for the alcoholic's or substance abuser's addiction. Just because the enabler's behavior has contributed to the maintenance of the addiction and changing this behavior can facilitate helping does not imply that enablers control abusers — nor does it imply that enablers are ultimately responsible.

Many enablers do take responsibility for their loved one's substance abuse. By making enablers a crucial part of the alcoholic's or addict's treatment, the therapist sends a clear message that the therapist also believes the enablers are responsible. Such a message may only increase the enabler's guilt and intensify their efforts to get their loved one to stop using. This may easily result in more of what they have done in the past.

It is most important that enablers and other family members are brought into treatment for *their own* relief and help and not as part of a scheme to change the addicted one. This is extremely difficult for the therapist to maneuver, for the following reasons. Once the enabler stops supporting, rescuing, tolerating or denying the alcoholism or drug-abuse problem, the alcoholic and drug abuser will no longer be protected from the natural consequences and punishments of addiction and abuse. Once this happens, the alcoholic and drug abuser will be more likely to pay the price for their abuse and things in their life will really start to go wrong. Once things start to go wrong they will probably cope by drinking or using drugs more. Then more natural consequences will occur. A downward spiral of crisis and drunkenness will follow. After this has occurred, the alcoholic and drug addict may "hit bottom". Most people in the drug- and alcoholism-treatment field believe that hitting bottom is good and may be the first step to recovery (Alcoholics Anonymous, 1984). The abuser can no longer deny the problem and will be motivated to stop drinking or using drugs by the pain of hitting bottom. As this downward spiral is started by with-drawal of the enabler's support – enablers can help the person to start the road to recovery by allowing this to occur. Unfortunately this can enhance their feeling of responsibility. Since the withdrawal of the enabler's support started the downward spiral – he or she can stop it by again giving support. If the enabler is overwhelmed by guilt, fear, jealousy, or other disturbed emotions when the alcoholic or drug addict suffers, he or she may end own emotional disturbance by rescuing the alcoholic or drug addict and again be caught in the role of an enabler.

We suggest that the therapist handle this issue in the following ways:

1. Enablers can be brought to the realization that their efforts to rescue their loved ones have not helped change them. This may be accompl-

ished by persistently and continually reviewing the pattern of events in the relationship. They can be persuaded that if they do want to help the alcoholic or drug user stop, the best thing *they* can do is *stop enabling*.
2. They can be helped to understand that this will probably start the downward spiral and make things worse for the alcoholic or drug user in the short term.
3. They can be helped to understand that there is *no guarantee* that precipitating a downward spiral will be the first step on the road to recovery for the addicted loved one. It is, however, the best option they have to help. Anything else they do is likely to support the addiction.
4. They can be helped to accept that there is always the risk that the alcoholic or loved one could spiral downward and stay there. A new, permanent level of low functioning could be reached.
5. Enablers can be helped to decide to stop supporting, denying, and tolerating the problem in light of the benefits such a change will bring to *their lives*. They can be made aware of all the benefits to them (and the rest of the family) if they stop the enabling role. Continuing in the enabling role will not help the addicted loved one and will keep them (and the rest of the family) in the present level of pain and suffering. Giving up the enabling role may help their addicted loved one and is likely to benefit them and other family members as well. Do they choose to sacrifice the possible benefit to the rest of the family to maintain the alcoholic or drug addict's present level of use or to prevent the alcoholic or drug addict from reaching lower levels of functioning? This can be accomplished by persistently and forcefully pointing out the benefits likely to follow if they abandon the enabling roles. The enablers are motivated to rescue the alcoholic or drug addict to relieve their own disturbed emotions. They can learn a better way to remove these disturbed feelings — namely, identifying and challenging the irrational beliefs that caused the disturbed emotions.

Once these steps have been taken, many will decide to give up their enabling role. However, the vast majority will be unable to follow through on carrying out the path that they know is the best for everyone. The fifth and final step is the most difficult. We shall now review the most common irrational beliefs of enablers.

IRRATIONAL BELIEFS OF ENABLING SPOUSES

Rational-emotive theory maintains that most individuals who remain in destructive relationships with alcoholics or drug addicts do so because they have disturbed negative emotions that prevent them from leaving or renegotiating the unsatisfying relationship. Many theorists and clinicians hypothesize that enablers are codependent on alcohol and drugs (Brown, 1985). This notion suggests the spouse chose a mate who had an alcohol or drug problem because the mate had the addiction or because they have some unconscious need to have the alcoholic stay addicted.

We do not find the concept of codependence helpful — for several reasons. The first is that many enablers chose their mates before an addiction developed. This makes it difficult to test a concept of codependence. Despite our dislike of the term *codependent*, clinical experience indicates that many individuals do go from one individual who drinks to another. Certainly someone who has repeatedly become involved with lovers or spouses who have drinking or drug problems is engaging in self-destructive behavior. Clinical experience also indicates that some individuals refuse to leave a hopeless destructive relationship with an alcoholic or drug abusing individual. The analogue of an addiction to a person or role can be recognized as having some validity. These enablers usually enter the joiner or silent sufferer roles.

Self-Worth and Need for Love

Rational-emotive theory hypothesizes that some individuals continually enter into and stay in relationships with alcoholics or drug addicts because they have an extreme fear of being alone and maintain the irrational belief that they do not deserve anything better. Because they believe they are worthless human beings, and no one good will have them, they are suspicious of entering any relationship in which they are treated well. If they do find such a relationship, they are sure they will be rejected as soon as their worthwhile partner discovers how worthless they really are. When they do enter a relationship with an alcoholic or drug addict they feel secure, for at least someone who treats them badly knows what a worthless person they are and continues in the relationship. They won't be left alone. They may believe that an alcoholic needs them, and if they are needed they won't be left. They also think that even a bad relationship is better than *no* relationship. Therefore, they will tolerate all sorts of abuse because they desperately need to be with someone and couldn't bear being alone.

Therapy with these individuals best focuses directly on the self-worth and need for love issues. The rational therapist would dispute the irrational belief that these clients are worthless people and must therefore settle for being treated poorly and that they could not bear being alone if they ever managed to break free of the present relationship. It is usually best to work on the self-worth issue first, and once self-acceptance is attained, the issue of being alone can be addressed. Once these individuals can imagine themselves functioning and living alone, they are ready to try to renegotiate their present relationship. They will probably also require help in developing assertion skills, problem-solving skills, and negotiating skills. The reason these enablers had better learn to be able to stand alone before they renegotiate the relationship is that the alcoholic and drug abuser will often threaten leaving — or even not come home — as a way of terrorizing these enablers into submission. At this point the enablers may require booster sessions and all the therapy techniques you can teach them to challenge their fears of abandonment. They can resist collapsing at this crisis. They have a chance to renegotiate the relationship.

If the relationship ends, the therapist's job is not over. Because of these clients' dire need for love and their chronic self-downing, they will be tempted to find another relationship like the last one. It is best for them to remain in therapy through their courtships with several new lovers to ensure that (a) they do not grab the first bad mate who will have them; (b) they learn to be choosy—that is, find a mate that they like, and (c) they maintain the belief that they are as worthwhile as anyone else and that they deserve to find a mate whom they enjoy. This could prevent them resorting to becoming an enabler once again.

Demands for Control

Enablers who take in a messianic role in the relationship are likely to believe that they are primarily responsible for the alcoholic's or drug addict's recovery. They demand that they have control over the behavior of their mate, and regardless of how often their partners relapse they will keep trying and never surrender — they must control them. Frequently enablers who fit this pattern have other irrational beliefs that endow them with noble stature for taking on such a Herculean task. These enablers may believe that they must take responsibility for their partner's substance abuse to show their love for their partner. The more abuse they take in the relationship or the more times they rescue the alcoholic, or the more times they try to get their mates to stop drinking — the more they prove their love for their mates. A variation on this irrational belief is that the more they suffer from the alcoholic, the more they sacrifice in rescuing the alcoholic, or the more they try to stop the alcoholic from drinking — the more they prove their nobility or superior worth.

Therapy with these individuals had best focus on dispelling their grandiose perception of responsibility and control. No one can control others behavior. No matter how hard these enablers try, or how noble their efforts are, the alcoholics or addicts control their own behavior. This point may have to be repeated hundreds of times before it is understood. It may also be helpful to have these enablers list all their attempts at ending their mate's drinking — empirically recording the failure of their many efforts may drive home the point.

A major disputing strategy for this group is to review what they get out of the relationship. Is their relationship based on reciprocal benefits to both parties? They actually behave as parents to the alcoholic's or drug user's role as child. The only gratification the enablers derive is from the relationship, that is, from the gratification of their neurotic need to control or parent. They may not get many or any other rewards that people usually seek from a romantic relationship. Does the gratification of *failing* to control actually make up for all the other lost aspects of enabling: What does the enabler risk if they give up their responsibility to control and just enjoy a relationship? What do they lose in self-esteem and self-worth if they no longer play this heroic role? Again, teaching self-acceptance to enablers will help them give up their futile role.

IRRATIONAL BELIEFS OF ENABLING PARENTS

Parents of alcoholics or drug abusers frequently engage in enabling their late adolescent or young adult children in more open and obvious ways than do spouses or lovers. Parents are much more likely to give gifts of money to cover unpaid bills that result from their children's lack of work or their expenditures on drugs. Parents are much more likely to hire attorneys to rescue their children from the legal consequences of drunk driving, assault, or drug trafficking. Parents are likely to provide housing and other necessities while the alcoholic or drug user fails to work. Parents are much more likely to believe that they are doing these things for the good of their children. Parents are less likely to see the relationship between their helping behaviors and their child's alcohol or drug abuse. Parents are less likely to believe that they benefit in any way from ceasing their enabling. If they do not rescue their child from the consequences of alcohol or drug abuse, they will only suffer and cover the suffering of their children as they start the downward spiral toward hitting bottom.

For these reasons, the therapist may need to be didactic and educational in helping parents of abusers learn how their helpfulness actually helps maintain their child's addiction. Parents are less likely to believe that they will benefit or improve their life by stopping their enabling role. They will often retort that such arguments are irrelevant for they are parents and they will bear any suffering necessary to help their children go straight. The only argument that works for such parents to give up their role is an authoritative stance by the therapist that the parent's only chance of having any positive influence on their children is to stop rescuing the child. The rescuing only continues the problem — they will suffer a lot watching their child hit bottom when they cease rescuing, but they can endure their discomfort to help their offspring. Once the parents accept this fact they still are prone to rescue their children from hitting bottom because of their disturbed emotions. These emotions are usually ego anxiety, discomfort anxiety, or guilt (DiGiuseppe, 1983, in press).

Those parents suffering ego anxiety are likely to believe that their worth as a human being is determined by how their children turn out. If the child has problems, they were bad parents and errors in parenting are unforgivable and make one an unworthy person (DiGiuseppe, 1983, in press). This belief can be attacked both empirically and philosophically. Empirically one can challenge that anyone is totally responsible for the way a person developed and may influence or have influenced their children. Philosophically they can learn how to accept themselves as persons regardless of what the outcome of their work is.

Parents who suffer discomfort anxiety often believe that the effort of forcing an intervention with their children is *too* difficult and that they are too weak to stand the pain of either seeing their children suffer or tolerating their children's behavior when the intervention is implemented (DiGiuseppe 1983, in press).

A variation on the low-frustration-tolerance belief is the parents' belief that their children are too fragile to stand being confronted with their alcohol or drug abuse, or too fragile to stand the process of detoxification or denial of their desires (DiGiuseppe, 1983, in press). These parents usually believe that if they confront their children with an intervention or if they stop enabling, their children will suffer some horrible emotional disturbance from which they will never recover. But what worse could happen to their children than already has? It is important to dispute not only the parents' low-frustration cognition but also their belief in their children's inability to tolerate frustration.

Chapter 11
RET in a Therapeutic Community

The most comprehensive and systematic form of treatment for drug and alcohol abusers is the Therapeutic Community. The Therapeutic Community is a microcosm of society. It is a self-contained and highly structured full-time therapeutic program offering rehabilitation for drug and alcohol abuse and general life enrichment

As members of the Therapeutic Community, residents form a strong therapeutic and emotional support system. They receive group and individual psychotherapy, develop job skills, complete their General High School Equivalency Diplomas, learn responsibility, and develop greater socialization skills. With progress and growth, and in a systematic step-by-step fashion, residents who had been unable to function in society previously are slowly prepared for reentry. As they meet specific goals in adaptive behavior, residents qualify for advanced levels of societal responsibility.

This chapter will show how the principles of Rational-Emotive Therapy can be effectively applied and integrated into the structure of a therapeutic community that totally integrates the rational-emotive model.

A PURE AND CONSISTENT MODEL

It is extremely important for a consistent approach to pervade the Therapeutic Community. This ensures that all residents learn the same materials, facilitates the modeling, and effects and unites the community with common tools in a common endeavor. Application of theoretically competing or opposing emphases is likely to divide the community, confuse the residents, and dilute treatment. If two or more theoretical approaches were employed within the same house, residents would be getting mixed messages about what they should do to help themselves. They would also be less likely to practice disputing of their irrational beliefs and negatively affect the staff's and the program's credibility in terms of perceived effectiveness.

Rational-emotive therapy offers residents of the Therapeutic Community an active, here-and-now oriented strategy and philosophy, which encourages them to take responsibility both for their pasts and for change (Ellis & Harper, 1975; Dryden, 1984; Walen, DiGiuseppe & Wessler, 1980; Wessler & Wessler, 1980). It does not emphasize palliative measures, but rather emphasizes helping clients make philosophic or characterological changes in thinking. This involves having them confront stressors and *work* at changing their thinking and behaving. It encourages acceptance of the consequences of one's own actions and tolerating uncomfortable circumstances. Although residents would likely prefer a comfortable and comforting treatment approach (because they typically avoid responsibilities, baby themselves and seek easy short-run-oriented solutions to problems), the Therapeutic Community implements that which is in the resident's best interest, not what interests them. The result is that they will likely experience much discomfort, tolerate it, and get on the road to recovery.

Considering the discomfort associated with implementing responsible and directive therapeutic interventions, the resident is likely to "do that which she or he knows best" in avoiding having to work at treatment. If an enabling, past-oriented or unconscious-oriented brand of therapy were available from some of the Therapeutic Community staff, residents would likely flock to it. It is highly doubtful that they would commit themselves to actually *working* at getting help, helping others, and helping themselves if a cushiony alternative modality were available. The substance abuser will even admit that she or he would rather take the easy way out. The substance abuser or alcoholic would also, however, admit that the easier way would not likely benefit them. In their more reasonable moments, residents do admit that they have confidence in the RET approach, admit that their "natural" or ingrained tendencies are to deny responsibility for their problems or for change and that, although they know that it would be better for them to take an active role in their rehabilitation, they would likely copout and lean toward a copout type of approach.

ENTERING THE THERAPEUTIC COMMUNITY

Chemically dependent persons rarely enter treatment voluntarily. When they do enter, it is usually because they have hit bottom, can no longer survive on the streets without a job, or have been thrown out of their homes by their parents, families, or landlords. Many are also court referred or are released from psychiatric hospitals. Some, however, do see the "errors of their ways," but this is the exception rather than the rule.

New residents are likely to say they are strongly motivated to receive help from a Therapeutic Community. They passively want to *receive* treatment: not getting it through their own efforts, but by having it come *to* them. They are not likely to believe that in order for them to change they will have to work, and work hard! Before entering the therapeutic community, the substance abuser has religiously avoided any and all of life's discomforts, challenges, and responsibilities. Therefore, when faced with stressors or discomfort, he or she typically and quickly gets high as a means to prevent any short-term discomfort or hassle. Because substance abusers have abysmally low tolerance for frustration or discomfort and are well practiced at avoiding circumstances where they may become even mildly distressed, the therapeutic regimen had better work to increase their tolerance levels and teach them more appropriate coping skills. These are the primary goals of the RET-based Therapeutic Community.

Therapeutic Communities offer residents a step-by-step program through which they learn to tolerate the frustration and hassles of daily life. Residents progress through increasingly more difficult *"levels"* of the program where each level requires the resident to perform more responsibilities and confronts the resident with incrementally more difficult stressors (or activating events). Because residents cannot escape, avoid or turn off these activating events unless they leave the program, they must face them and learn to deal with them. An example of how the structure of the therapeutic community helps activate the residents irrational beliefs is presented in Figure 11.1.

THE COMMUNITY

Positive peer pressure pervades the Therapeutic Community and serves several purposes. First, residents hold their peers accountable for their behaviors. While positive, self-enhancing attitudes and behaviors are reinforced with acceptance and approval, negative "street" attitudes and behaviors are discouraged. Learning experiences and negative consequences await those who display these negatives.

Residents regularly "blow the whistle" on their peers for displaying negative attitudes or behaviors. They do this to help their peers learn that their behaviors are not acceptable within this, or any, community. Because the residents are themselves street smart, they are very talented at detecting the cons and manipulations of their peers. Since they are

Figure 11.1.
Irrational Ideas Leading to Drug and Alcohol Abuse:
Discomfort Anxiety

A = House rules
     Responsibilities
RB = I don't like hassles
*IB = Therefore, I should not have to deal with them
     I can't stand hassles
     I can't stand discomfort
C = Frustration
     Anger
     Depression
RB = I do not like feeling discomfort
*IB = I can't stand discomfort
     it is *too* hard to tolerate
     I shouldn't have to stand it
Cb (old) Drugs and/or alcohol are used to turn off the discomfort the individual
          thinks is *intolerable*
Cb (new) The resident is prevented from using drugs and can not avoid
          responsibilities in the community, but learns more appropriate cognitions,
          disrupting strategies and behaviors. The resident learns that discomfort can
          be tolerated.

Key:
A = activating event
RB = rational belief
IB = irrational belief
C = consequence
Cb = behavioral consequence

dedicated to helping themselves and their peers change, and since they themselves will receive negative consequences if they do not blow their whistles, they prevent their peers from "getting over".

Blowing the whistle on a friend or peer is a very stressful and powerful Activating Event for residents. In doing so, however, they overcome their irrational needs for approval and comfort. This also reinforces their commitment to change and their value of positive images.

Positive peer pressure also serves to strip residents of their street images. Residents are not likely to be motivated to change things about themselves. It is much easier to avoid responsibilities and get high all day. However, residents of the community reinforce only positive, rational, goal-directed and self-help-directed attitudes and behaviors. If a resident is to receive any social reinforcement, it is only through displaying appropriate attitudes and behaviors. Residents chastise and attack negativity and irrational thinking because they are aware of its potential damages. They work to help their peers get free of their irrationalities and self-defeating behaviors.

Peer pressure in the form of positive modelling is also quite powerful. As residents consistently apply and encourage rational attitudes and appropriate behaviors, new residents' preconceived notions that cool people do not think or act positively is disputed. In fact, residents learn from how they see other residents acting. This is why it is especially important for residents to exhibit rational attitudes and teach it to their peers. Residents show others that it is okay to admit that you have problems, to show your faults, to open up to others, and to admit that you need and want help.

Residents are also held accountable by random urinalysis and strip searches. If their urine comes up "dirty" or if drugs or drug paraphernalia are found on them or in their rooms, they experience loss of privileges, extra work assignments, demotion, or other negative consequences. Their parole or probation officers might also be notified. It is important to *not* allow the residents to get over on the program.

HOW A THERAPEUTIC COMMUNITY TEACHES

Therapeutic Community teaches residents how to apply program material and dispute irrational beliefs through several modalities. Residents are taught didactically, through experience and through modeling.

Residents learn much of the therapeutic material through didactic means. They are given books, pamphlets, and other materials to read; they watch specifically selected videotapes; and they are specifically taught by other staff, guest speakers, other residents, and their house mates.

Modeling (Bandura, 1977) plays a major part in the therapeutic process. Residents directly and indirectly show each other how to think and act differently, and in more rational and self-enhancing ways. Then one philosophy, that of rational-emotive therapy, pervades the Therapeutic Community, residents consistently see how they had better think and act if they want to help themselves and live long, happy and productive lives.

Much of the learning that occurs in the Therapeutic Community is done through experience. Residents are given assignments and mini-experiments to test out new ways of thinking (Beck, Rush, Shaw, & Emery, 1979). They might give a seminar to the entire house on, for example, why they do not need to be comfortable all the time and how they can stand hassles. Or they might be asked to write a composition on an RET principle they are having difficulty understanding or applying. Residents are continually forced to apply program material.

Since the Therapeutic Community is highly structured and prevents residents from escaping or avoiding the stressful activating events inherent in any sort of community life, residents are frequently quite distressed. They are, therefore, given many opportunities to apply coping and disputational strategies in vivo. Rational thinking is both positively and negatively reinforced for the resident, in that it leads to more productive and pleasurable emotions and behavior and serves to turn off any inappropriate and negative feelings (Craighead, Kazdin, & Mahoney, 1981).

By having residents at all levels in one community, any particular resident can not say realistically that the program is *too hard* or that it *causes* them distress. After all, other residents have moved through it successfully. This proves that although it might be *hard*, it is not *too hard* and gives staff and other residents good opportunities to help residents dispute their notions that they can not stand unpleasantness and acknowledge that it is their thinking and not the program that upsets them. The staff could then convince the residents that they would benefit by changing their ways of thinking, identify their respective irrational beliefs, challenge and dispute their faulty ways of thinking and subsequently think in more rational, selfenhancing and goal-producing ways.

House Rules and Contracts Must Be Fair

The reality of the Therapeutic Community is like that of the real world. Residents are often likely to feel much aggravation and frustration as a result of their demands that the house (and the world's) rules be fair. On the outside, the substance abuser would escape perceived unfairness by using drugs, alcohol, or aggression. Within the Therapeutic Community, however, the substance abuser has no power in changing, escaping or avoiding those activating events that are often perceived as unfair. The resident must, therefore, face that which she or he deems unfair.

If residents continually upset themselves by demanding fairness, they will continue feeling miserable, will undoubtedly lose their house privileges, and will impede their progress through the treatment levels. They are, therefore, confronted with the decision to continue in their no-win situations or give up the notion that they can't stand unfairness.

Peer pressure facilitates residents accepting that unfairness will *always* likely exist. Staff and other residents point out the parallel with the outside world — which is likely to be at least as unfair. It is in everyone's best interest to just accept this as a fact of life.

Residents are also likely to believe that treatment is supposed to be easy and comfortable. This is often related to their thoughts of themselves as special persons. They are soon taught, especially by their peers, that they do not rule this or any other universe and that, even if mommy and daddy might have made life comfortable for them, it didn't really help them. They still became a drug addict. Even if the residents do not at first change their philosophies about comfort, they are at least willing to act as if they have. Behavior change is a good first step.

IMPATIENCE

Most residents think that they cannot wait to move up to the next higher level or that they need to finish the program immediately. They typically believe that they *can't* wait or that they *should not have to* wait for things. They believe that they *need* what they want when they want it. In the Therapeutic Community, however, the residents almost invariably will not get their demands satisfied, especially within the demanded time limit. The resident therefore learns through experience to delay gratification and stand the wait.

Many of the residents' demands to get through the program quickly are the result of their comparing their own rates of advancement with those of others. Residents tend to think dichotomously and tend to equate slow progress with no progress. They may also make their self-worth contingent upon the degree to which their efforts at self-help are recognized by staff and others. Besides helping the residents give up their irrational beliefs, which cause their impatience, treatment emphasizes self-acceptance, which is neither contingent upon the approval of others nor on rate of advancement.

THE PAST

Once residents have detoxed, they often experience extreme guilt, condemning themselves for hurting others and for their own failures and misdeeds. They tend to consider themselves as worthless and unforgivable, and believe that they are destined to be losers. Therapy, therefore, focuses on helping them accept themselves with their past and current problems, and on moving on toward a brighter future. They are not encouraged to *forget* their pasts, because that would prevent them from learning from their previous mistakes. Rather, they are taught to *forgive* themselves.

CONTINGENT REINFORCERS

Residents do not have free rewards or privileges. In fact, their treatment is geared toward helping them appreciate that life's rewards are not free but, rather, are *earned* through positive efforts. There is no "free lunch". By having to earn their privileges, residents learn to delay gratification, work for life's rewards and not demand that they get privileges noncontingently. While in the Therapeutic Community, and likely while in outside society, substance abusers can demand and expect all that they want. Considering the way both the Therapeutic Community and society are structured, however, rewards are not likely to come noncontingently. Therefore, if the residents are to tolerate life's cruel realities and handle life's disappointments drug free, they had better give up their demands about what life *owes* them.

LOW FRUSTRATION TOLERANCE/
LOW TOLERANCE FOR
DISCOMFORT

The most predominant irrational belief among substance abusers is that they *cannot stand discomfort*. In order to learn to tolerate discomfort, one must first be exposed to it. However, without the imposed structure of the Therapeutic Community, which requires exposure to discomfort and which prevents them from escaping it inappropriately, the resident would not likely get over this discomfort anxiety. With exposure and the challenging of their irrationhal beliefs, residents learn that although they would prefer life to be stress free, it will not likely be so. Therefore, they had better face life's stressors and learn that they are, in fact, bearable.

Poor, Poor, Pitiful Me

Faced with the challenge to change, residents struggle with their tendencies to feel pitifully sorry for themselves. To combat the poor-poor-me syndrome, staff and other residents force self-pitiers to keep active and to attack the irrational beliefs by writing compositions disputing the notion that they are hopeless cases, or by giving seminars in front of the entire house describing why there is hope for everyone even though you might not always see it. Also, if a resident thinks that he or she can't help being depressed, he or she is allowed to do so but only in confined areas. Such a resident may be given a "mope chair" which is placed in a position so that the resident does not get any attention from his peers while feeling sorry for himself or herself. This is done in the case where it is suspected that there is some secondary gain received as a result of this moping.

THE VALUE OF A STEP-BY-STEP REHABILITATION

Progress through the various levels of the Therapeutic Community presents numerous and varied activating events to residents. Duties and responsibilities increase in number and complexity; pressures and expectations from other residents increase regarding a variety of issues; and discomfort and frustration increase with movement through subsequent levels. Also, whereas privileges are more plentiful at each level, residents have more to lose if they are demoted to a lower level. There is no doubt that pressure and discomfort increase with increasing levels. This process ensures that they get an opportunity to use cognitive disputing at any activating event about which they might upset themselves. Thus, there are no surprises to the client or the therapist when the resident reenters society; they have been faced with every type of stressor they might face in the real world and have had practice disputing the irrational beliefs any such event might elicit in them.

Substance abusers typically have abysmally low tolerance levels for frustration and discomfort. In addition, their tendencies are to think of themselves as inadequate and incapable of making any changes in their lives. Many also have quite grandiose ideas, thinking that they know how to take care of themselves and do not need help. Substance abusers are also likely to blame others and even society at large for their discomforts. They do not accept the responsibility for their actions and they often do not see their negative, self-defeating behaviors as harmful to themselves or society. Often, too, they just do not care.

Moving through subsequent levels of the Therapeutic Community, residents learn to cope and tolerate increasing levels of discomfort. Through disputing their irrational beliefs at each level, they learn that they can handle what may seem as unbearable pressures or responsibilities, and can tolerate what they perceive as unfair, capriciously dispersed negative consequences. As they continually experience discomforts they are not permitted to avoid or escape, and since they did not die from previous discomfort, residents learn that they *can stand* discomfort and hassles. They also learn that they *can stand* unfairness and that it really is *not that bad* and it is *not intolerable* when things do not go the way they would like. Previous experiences within the Therapeutic Community can act as potent behavioral disputes of residents' irrational beliefs.

A Therapeutic Community teaches residents to admit their problems. By continually experiencing frustration and discomfort in the program, and since they can no longer just turn off their pain with drugs or alcohol, residents come to realize the extent of their addiction or dependence on substances. It is at this point that they are likely to admit that they have a problem and are willing to change their faulty ways of thinking and learn alternative coping skills.

A Therapeutic Community teaches residents that they can be competent. As residents master the responsibilities at subsequent levels of the treatment program, they are not only reinforced for their progress and efforts with increased privileges, but also learn that they have the capacity to do well at some things and are actually more competent than they would likely give themselves credit for being. They learn that they can, therefore, make an impact in life and that their efforts can, and do, pay off. Thoughts of hopelessness, helplessness, and worthlessness are thus disputed (Beck, 1976; Beck, Rush, Shaw, & Emery, 1979). With mastery of responsibilities often comes a change in residents' thinking about responsibilities. Residents start to appreciate and value achievement and take active interest in various activities and vocations. The apathy with which they enter the Therapeutic Community dissipates with skill mastery (Seligman, 1975).

As residents move through the levels of the program, they also play a greater role in the rehabilitation of their residence peers. They help each other through crises, in learning program material, in developing new attitudes and better coping skills and in handling pressures and frustrations. Their thoughts that they are alone in the world, that it is useless to care for anyone, and that no one cares about them are changed in this regard. The value of the community plays a major part in the rehabilitation process.

LEVELS OF THE THERAPEUTIC COMMUNITY

As was previously stated, residents of a Therapeutic Community proceed through progressively difficult and challenging levels en route to completing treatment and reentering society. Advancement through progressive steps is overseen by staff, who function in both supportive and therapeutic roles. Residents' responsibilities at each level are tailored to their individual levels of functioning, which is determined through formal assessment and case conferencing. They must demonstrate mastery and competence at each level in order to advance. The time to complete each level is, therefore, individual and specific.

The following will be a description of the levels of the Therapeutic Community as they operate at a specific program which use the RET approach.

Orientation

Upon entering the Therapeutic Community, residents are in the orientation level. As the name implies, they are oriented to the rules they must follow in order to remain a resident of the community. During orientation, residents are engaged in numerous activities in learning program material. The emphasis at this stage of treatment is to get them integrated and accepting of their new family and community. This is accomplished through attending nightly meetings where they get to know other residents, being assigned a House Mate, who teaches them the ropes, and by the support, encouragement, and warmth they receive from other residents during this most difficult time.

Residents also engage in discussions of drugs and alcohol and their psychological, physiological, and social effects. A determined effort is made to keep orientation-level residents extremely busy, getting them immersed in house functions and seeing that other members of the house are available to them in a strong support system. This is found to be extremely important in increasing the likelihood that the new resident, who is likely detoxing from addiction, will remain in treatment.

At the orientation level, the residents have *no* privileges. They are not permitted to receive visitors, to make telephone calls, to listen to the radio, to smoke cigarettes in their rooms, or to date. They are searched each time they reenter the community. The purpose of withholding these privileges is to focus the residents' entire energies on learning program material. Not having the privileges also provides many activating events for them to experience discomfort anxiety. The loss of free privileges also denies them activities that could be used as distractors. In this way they will have to learn program materials and disputing strategies as coping skills. The lack of privileges provides many opportunities to apply and practice disputing.

Residents also learn the importance of following rules. Substance abusers usually try to bend rules and fail to meet social responsibilities. RET has always taught that people will be happier and better adjusted if they agree to follow social contracts (Ellis, 1973a; Ellis & Becker, 1982; Walen, DiGiuseppe & Wessler, 1980). In order to get the benefits of a social contract (with one's mate, family or friends) one best keeps the responsibilities of the contract. The Therapeutic Community stresses that a resident must follow the rules of the community in order to get the benefits of the community membership. It is not acceptable to copout of one's responsibilities because the responsibilities are *too* difficult and still get the benefits from the community. All residents will be held responsible for their attitudes and behavior.

In orientation, residents also learn the meaning of rehabilitation. They learn that rehabilitation is an unending process and that, in order for them to benefit from the program and become drug free and enrich their lives, they had better give up (a) their demands for comfort, (b) their negative self-downing beliefs, (c) their street attitudes, and (d) their resistance to follow house procedure. All residents must also give consent to submit to random urinalysis. When the resident understands the house rules and the workings of the community, the resident may advance to Level One. Orientation may last for approximately 4 to 8 weeks, depending on the particular resident.

Level One

The foundation for the rehabilitation process is laid at Level One. Residents learn how to apply what the program calls the "tools" of: 1) humility, 2) truthfulness, 3) honesty, 4) sincerity, and 5) responsibility. They also learn what are termed the 3 D's, namely: 1) determination 2) goal-direction, and 3) discipline. Essentially, the 5 tools and the 3 D's help the resident endorse a new and therapeutically more beneficial philosophy about the treatment process and about life in general.

It is important for residents to learn humility. In learning humility, they learn to admit that they have problems and are not able to solve them on their own. Residents develop the ability to reach out and ask for help and to stand the discomfort associated with admitting one's faults. They learn to accept themselves as fallible human beings. Residents develop the ability to admit that they are not special human beings and admit that the world and universe does not owe them special contingencies or privileges. They learn to tolerate society's imposed rules and sanctions and accept that the world does not owe them favors or free-lunch.

To apply the tools of honesty and truthfulness, residents must develop an attitude of accepting the consequences of their behavior and realizing that they can, in fact, tolerate the consequences of being honest and truthful to themselves and others. They also learn that the long-term consequences of dishonesty are worse. Truthfulness is considered to be the thought process and honesty is the action of being truthful. For RET to be effective, residents learn to be truthful and honest to themselves and others in order to recognize and admit their irrationalities. These tools help the drug addicts and alcoholics realize the frequency with which they lie to themselves and others and helps them to correct this.

Residents also learn sincerity. They learn that they do not need to be defensive and deny their feelings and pains. They see that they can tolerate the discomfort of admitting their emotions and they develop the ability to keep committed to themselves and others.

Responsibility is developed when the residents realize and incorporates that it is in their own best interest to engage in social contracts which require giving in order to get. They recognize that they are answerable and accountable for their choices, decisions, and actions and learn not to project blame on either their parents, the world or their pasts. They also learn to stand the discomfort associated with living up to their responsibilities in life, in making changes in oneself, and in accepting constructive criticism.

Determination is fostered by helping the resident realize that hard work is required to beat one's addiction and to achieve one's goals in life. Residents learn that it need not be easy and they had better accept that discomfort is a part of changing, growing, and achieving.

Residents are also taught to be goal directed, to choose realistic and positive goals, and to not demand that pursuit of them be easy or free of hassle.

Discipline and commitment to one's goals are also sought. Residents learn that despite obstacles and discomfort, they can still persist.

In moving from Orientation Level to Level One, residents earn the privilege to receive in-house visits. These privileges, however, are contingent upon the resident's consistently displaying application of house principles. Residents have to earn their visits by participating and working in individual and group therapy sessions and by maintaining at least cordial relations with other members of the community. Because it is *unlikely* that the Level One residents will have internalized a more rational, self-enhancing philosophy in the brief time within the community, they are reinforced for *acting as if* they have. Here effort and faith in the material is reinforced and the theory is that behavior change may facilitate cognitive change. Residents learn that they can control their *behavior* even if they are *feeling* badly. They learn that their *feelings* do not have to dictate how you *act*. They see how to tolerate their negative feelings, not saying to themselves that they can't stand feeling badly and therefore drink or take drugs. Rather, they learn social problem-solving skills, coping strategies, assertiveness, and relaxation in order to *control their behavior regardless of how they feel*.

Residents can receive visitors only when the visitor is believed to be acceptable by a screening committee. Acceptability is based on interview data and upon analysis of a urine specimen. Residents are not permitted to have visitors, even if they are family members, if the visitor's urine is "dirty". Residents are prevented from associating with people who use or abuse drugs or alcohol.

To meet their responsibility to be a productive member of the community, Level One residents are assigned relatively simple duties. For example, they may be assigned to a clean-up crew, a kitchen crew, or a laundry crew, or may assist in keeping the resident census (which monitors where each resident is at all times). Level One residents may also serve as House Mate to an Orientation Level resident, teaching the rules of the community and so forth.

As is true at all levels, Level One residents receive pressure from upper level residents to work at helping themselves. Residents have increasing expectations placed on them in terms of performing house chores and duties and in better managing their emotions. The Level One resident is presented with very potent activating events with which the resident has typically used drugs and alcohol to deal. The residents' beliefs that they can't stand hassles, that they should not have to stand hassles, and that they can't stand the discomfort associated with hassles become most obvious at this stage.

In the Therapeutic Community, residents are not permitted to shirk or avoid responsibilities and, of course, are not allowed to use drugs or alcohol to deal with them. They must, therefore, face responsibilities. They are encouraged and supported in learning to apply cognitive and behavioral strategies in order to cope with hassles and stressors. Upon becoming proficient at facing the discomforts, hassles, and responsibilities that they would normally avoid, the resident will have behaviorally and cognitively disputed many of their irrational notions. They come to see and believe that they can, in fact, stand discomfort and that they are actually more competent than they previously believed. Subsequent levels of the program offer increasingly difficult and stressful activating events, which the residents will learn to cope with and tolerate, thereby enhancing and reinforcing their new beliefs and attitudes.

The resident's ability to use RET principles to cope with these purposely imposed activating events are monitored by staff and upper level residents. The success or failure to use disputing then becomes the focus of that resident's work in group or individual therapy.

When the Level One resident has basically learned to apply the 5 tools and 3 Ds effectively, and is considered by the staff to be working hard to self-help, and has demonstrated the ability to better identify and manage emotions and responsibilities, the Level One resident can move up to the level of Supervisor. The move from Level One to Supervisor is based more on knowledge of program material than on actual functioning level. Knowledge of the material is the foundation upon which the remainder of treatment builds.

Supervisor Level

Increased privileges come with becoming a Supervisor. As Supervisors, residents have earned the right to live in nicer room accommodations (which comes with advancement), to smoke in their rooms, and to have visitors outside of the residence. Although these privileges are powerful motivators for Level One residents to strive for the Supervisor level, they also present many potentially stressful activating events.

While outside visits are indeed motivating and reinforcing, they often prove to be quite stressful. For the first time since entering the community, residents interact with people from outside the Therapeutic Community and people from their pasts. These visits often stir up emotions, ideas, and thoughts about how the resident has failed, how they can't stand living "inside," and how they have hurt their families. The visits also remind them of all the things they have lost as a result of their addictions.

Also, since they can have outside visits, they can resume (or begin) dating. Dating is usually a very potent activating event. Now the resident faces possible rejection, which unleashes a host of irrational beliefs. Residents are likely to think of themselves as incompetent, unlovable, unworthy, or as needing a loving relationship to make them complete. The substance abuser is not used to interacting socially in a drug-free environment or doing so without being high. Since the usual coping mechanisms (drugs) are not available, they must learn to socialize without chemical influence. This is the real test.

As a result of the irrational beliefs that are activated at the Supervisor Level, the resident is likely to experience some intense negative emotions. This provides new opportunities to practice disputing and provides much new material to be discussed in group and individual therapy.

Supervisors are also faced with increased responsibilities. Many of their responsibilities concern their interactions with lower level residents and their obligation to report on any of their subordinates or peers who display negative attitudes or behaviors. Supervisors inform upper level residents of any irregularities, so that appropriate consequences can be doled out. This obligation holds for all residents at all levels.

Irrational beliefs concerning need for approval and need for comfort tend to cause strong fears, which interfere with Supervisors' abilities to make their peers and subordinates accountable for their behaviors.

These beliefs are challenged at this level and more rational and responsible beliefs are developed. It is in the Supervisor's best interest to get over the belief that it is too hard to blow the whistle on a friend for negative behavior. If the whistle does not sound, the Supervisor is served consequences for neglecting duties.

Near the end of the Supervisor Level, a vocational assessment is conducted. Treatment is then also geared toward helping the resident develop the skills needed in outside the work force. As the Supervisor develops these skills, demonstrates responsible fulfillment of community duties, demonstrates ability to effectively manage emotions when faced with stressful activating events, and functions as a good leader and role model for subordinates, the Supervisor moves up to the level of Assistant Coordinator. Whereas the primary concern in determining whether a Level One resident can move up to Supervisor was the ability to merely demonstrate knowledge of program material, the movement to Assistant Coordinator involves an increased ability to *apply* the material.

Assistant Coordinator Level

At this level, residents gain the privilege of more visit hours and the right to carry money. These are powerful reinforcers and incentives for residents.

Assistant Coordinators have numerous responsibilities that require skill and judgment. These include: (a) determining appropriate consequences for the transgressions committed by their peers or residents at lower levels, (b) presenting these consequences to residents, and (c) designing behavioral contracts. Every contract, however, must be signed and approved by staff members. In pronouncing negative consequences or behavioral contracts in others, Assistant Coordinators face the strong possibility of being rejected, disliked or even hated. Their irrational beliefs regarding need for approval become most apparent. Also, any remaining tendency to avoid responsibility because it is too hard will come to the surface.

Assistant Coordinators also supervise the Supervisors. Many Assistant Coordinators are likely to demand that they do this *perfectly*. They believe that they should give good advice, guidance, and know-how, since they have advanced beyond the Supervisor Level. Assistant Coordinators also are likely to demand that the Supervisors perform their duties mistake free, and to condemn their subordinates when they have erred. They commonly believe that others should be punished when they make mistakes. Assistant Coordinator groups focus on helping Assistant Coordinators dispute these irrational demands and become more tolerant and accepting of their own and of others' faults.

Assistant Coordinators, who are directly supervised by staff group leaders, are also responsible for the efficiency of the house crews. They are in charge of clean-up, transportation, hot line coverage, the switchboard, bingo, and numerous other activities. They must also teach the program material to the lower level residents. They are, realistically, being pulled in numerous directions. The purpose is to give them real-life experiences at directing and operating the organization and to help them work at challenging and disputing the notion that their lives must be easy and that they must perform perfectly.

The extent to which Assistant Coordinators and other upper level residents advance through the program is a function of their meeting their vocational goals (developing certain skills, developing an interest in a particular vocational field, finding a job, etc.) and therapy goals (such as increasing frustration tolerance and self-acceptance), which are outlined in each resident's respective treatment plan.

House Coordinator

House Coordinators (Houses) have more pleasant living conditions and no longer need to be searched (as are residents at all levels below them) when they enter the residence. They have earned their privileges, have demonstrated their competencies, have made the requisite therapeutic gains, and are preparing themselves to run the residence when they reach Chief Coordinator — and ultimately to graduate from the program and reenter society. The activating events they face have to do with these two very powerfully reinforcing, yet potentially stressing events.

House Coordinators typically get quite nervous and stressed as a result of their thoughts about the nearing prospect of graduating from the program. They tend to predict failure outside the residence based on their perceived inadequacies. These anxieties tend to interfere with their house functions and responsibilities. This in turn activates their beliefs that it would be awful, or that it will prove that they are incompetent if they fail at the House Coordinator duties or if they are demoted back to Assistant Coordinator.

Ideally, and ultimately, House Coordinators learn to handle their responsibilities, better manage their emotions, and tolerate stress and discomfort. Their therapy also focuses heavily on their irrational beliefs about self-worth and their demands for success. If they demonstrate adequate emotional management, coping skills and ability to delegate decisions through the ranks, oversee contracts, complete and monitor paperwork without significant emotional agitation, the House Coordinator may be promoted to the next level.

Chief Coordinator

The Chief Coordinator has the most privileges. He or she has earned the most hours per visit and is also allowed to leave the house at approved times to see movies, attend sporting events or engage in other entertainments. With these privileges, as in the outside world, comes added responsibilities. The Chief Coordinator is the chief of the house and is ultimately responsible for all residence functions. She or he runs the house and is answerable to staff for everything that goes on. The Chief Coordinator is thus faced with various and sundry activating events.

The Chief Coordinator also faces closely pending reentry into society. Here many irrational beliefs begin to surface. Ideas that they must not show any sign of difficulty coping with their reentry (since, of course, they are the Chiefs), and that they must reenter society anxiety free and discomfort free, lead them to experience much distress. Negative predictions about their abilities to function in society are often made and the Chief is likely to make self-worth contingent upon success. Self-worth is therefore on the line. All of these issues are grist for the mill of group and individual therapy.

Once the Chief demonstrates that she or he can responsibly run the house, self-manage appropriately in spite of these potent activating events, and function effectively and responsibly outside of the house, then the Chief Coordinator is ready to move out and become more independent. Reentry most depends on the Chief Coordinator's ability to live independently. He or she must not only have developed the personal resources to function outside of the house but must also have developed an adequate and positive support system outside of the Therapeutic Community.

At this point, the Chief must write a thesis describing the treatment, its benefits, how she or he intends to continue in the self-rehabilitation process, and what her or his plans are. The thesis is supposed to demonstrate the resident's knowledge of the irrational beliefs that led to the addiction and what attitudes and behaviors were self-destructive. It must also demonstrate knowledge of which disputing and coping strategies work and are likely to keep her or him drug and/or alcohol free. Upon completion of an acceptable thesis, the Chief is approved to reenter society.

Reentry Level

Reentry is where the resident, having graduated from the program, becomes an outpatient. For the first 28 days of reentry, graduates give back to the program that which they took from it; namely, an armamentarium of coping strategies and a new, more rational and empirical philosophy about life. Reentry Level clients run groups and are available to the program residents to teach them program materials and RET and to help them with their problems. This serves to reinforce program materials and rational thinking in the heads of the Reentry clients.

Reentry clients face real-life stressors. They now confront in vivo those things that they typically escaped or avoided before treatment. They face getting and maintaining employment, going to school, establishing or reestablishing social relationships, reintegration into their families and living independently, responsibly, and selfsufficiently. It is at this level of rehabilitation that the clients get to apply what was learned in the residential program. What they needed drugs to handle prior to treatment they now handle clean. They continue in individual therapy to reinforce their disputing skills and help themselves identify new irrational beliefs and troublesome activating events they may not have mastered.

Reentering into society proper is the toughest test of the residents' new belief systems. During the in-house period of treatment they progress from day-one residents, who think of themselves as inadequate and hopeless, to Chief Coordinators, who have demonstrated their abilities to get their lives in positive order. Contrary to what they predict upon entering the program, residents become quite comfortable and safe within the Therapeutic Community. They develop respect and admiration from other members of the community and have become part of a community with shared values and goals. However, although the resident has grown within the self-contained community and has disputed his or her notions that he or she is worthless and that he or she cannot be helped, reentering society presents more real-life and stressful activating events.

The reentry clients usually enter the job market at the bottom of the totem pole. Although they have been prepared for these activating events, confronting them in vivo is a big step. These new activating events enter the forefront of reentry group and individual sessions, where clients learn to dispute their irrational beliefs about real-life issues.

GROUP THERAPY

All residents receive RET in groups at *each* level of the program. Group therapy focuses on helping residents develop more rational and self-enhancing beliefs and attitudes, not only to employ with regard to residence issues, but also regarding current concerns, past concerns and concerns regarding their reentries into society. The groups are active and directive and are both thematic and problem based. Therapists are always monitoring the resident's progress. A resident's emotional upsets, copouts, and failures to meet responsibilities are brought into each session. The therapist then helps the resident to identify the irrational beliefs, dispute these irrationalities, and develop new rational beliefs.

During both formal and informal staff meetings, group leaders and individual therapists share their insights into the irrational beliefs of the residents. This helps to ensure that at least someone will catch a particular resident when he or she is functioning through their irrational beliefs.

To personalize the group therapy and identify the particular irrational beliefs of each resident, various exercises and homework assignments are utilized. For example, residents are required to put into their own language each of Ellis' 10 irrational beliefs. They are also instructed to keep running logs of the situations where they got upset and record each irrational belief. In terms of relapse prevention, they are also made to think of situations in the future where specific irrational beliefs could operate and lead them back to drug or alcohol use or abuse. Group leaders set contingencies, both positive and negative, for completion of assignments. As a result, compliance is usually 100%.

Groups are often experiential in nature. Gestalt therapy techniques, such as the empty chair or hot seat, may be utilized where residents become emotionally aroused and are required to identify, dispute, and change the irrational beliefs that led to their upsets. They do not become aroused for the purpose of a reaction, but rather to bring their irrational ideas to the fore. Numerous imagery exercises, in vivo shame attacks, role-plays, and confrontational exercises also serve this purpose.

Establishing the Need for Help

Groups function to help residents set goals for themselves. Goals might be of an emotional, behavioral, attitudinal, interpersonal, familial, or vocational nature. Regardless, it is important for the residents to acknowledge and admit that they do have something toward which to work. If they do not, peer pressure and house contracts will convince them that they do. They come to see that the activating events in their lives are not likely to change, especially when they are residents of the Therapeutic Community.

B → C

The focus of group therapy is changing residents' beliefs about themselves, others, life in general, the past and the future. To demonstrate the relationship between thoughts and feelings, group leaders employ didactic teachings, bibliotherapy, experiential exercises, group discussions, and behavioral and written homework assignments. Experienced peers reflect how they are doing and feeling much better as a result of changes in their own thinking, thus modeling good RET skills. Since everyone in the house operates off of the principle that thoughts cause feelings, and since there are posters in various parts of the residence reinforcing this point, it becomes accepted as a way of life.

Changing the As while in the Therapeutic Community

Besides helping residents change their characteristic ways of thinking and relating in the world, the Therapeutic Community also serves to help residents change many of the negative situations or Activating Events in their lives. For example, they do learn job skills so that when they reenter society they are not faced with a difficult job market and/or unemployment. Also, they can earn their General Equivalency Diplomas within the Therapeutic Community so that the job search will be easier. Why not change the As when you can?

The Therapeutic Community also works to develop a positive support system for each resident upon reentry. The first step is to help the resident's family to function better. This is accomplished through family groups, which are run weekly while the resident is still in treatment. Family groups, like resident groups, are both theme and problem oriented. The general goal is to help family members develop some of the rational attitudes that the resident learned while in treatment and to subsequently increase mutual tolerance, respect, and communication among family members. Family members also learn how to consistently apply contingency management with the children and to not enable them in the future.

A positive reentry network is also encouraged during the resident's tenure in the Therapeutic Community. All visitors are screened by urinalysis and any potential relationship the resident wants to establish must be acceptable to staff according to certain criteria; therefore, the only relationships that will be waiting for the reentry graduates are considered to be drug free, positive, and appropriate.

Chapter 12
Therapist Survival Skills

Most professionals who work in the field of alcoholism and substance-abuse treatment agree that these clients can present many challenges and problems. Many practitioners we talk to at workshops tell us that they find it difficult to maintain a rational and objective attitude toward some of their clients, given the slow progress and the many demands on the practitioner these clients often make. The institutional and clinical settings in which clinical services are often delivered can further exacerbate therapy problems. For those of us who work with a large number of these "difficult customers" there may be a real issue of professional burnout.

In this final chapter we will develop some ideas and suggestions for those working with these clients that will help combat some of their difficulties. Certainly, working with these clients can be hard, but it is only "too hard" when we as therapists define it as such. To do the hard work required for effective RET with addicts, you can first develop a set of realistic and rational attitudes toward this work and then check yourself with ongoing self appraisal or self-supervision to see if you are staying on track.

THERAPIST ATTITUDES

As Ellis (1985a) has pointed out, we as therapists can be our own most difficult client and actually cause some of the difficulties we have in working with tough customers. We can upset ourselves with irrational beliefs about ourselves, our clients, their problems and the nature and outcome of our therapeutic work. When we do this, our resulting disturbed feelings interfere with effective performance, make our work far more difficult than it has to be, and ultimately may result in a progressive loss of regard for our clients and ourselves. When we afflict ourselves with this type of burnout, we model for our clients the very low frustration tolerance, demandingness, and discomfort avoidance we are ostensibly trying to help them change.

The most effective way to avoid being your own most difficult client is to learn to identify and work persistently to change your own irrationality about yourself, your clients, and your work. Look for implicit and explicit absolutistic "shoulds" you have for yourself and your clients. Persistently question these shoulds to help eliminate the disturbed affect that makes an already difficult job even more difficult. As fallible human beings, even the most rational of therapists (yes, even Albert Ellis!) will think irrationally on occasion. Pay attention to your dysfunctional feelings and behavior indicators of irrational thinking that require challenging. Once you have identified these ideas, challenge them persistently and often.

Ellis (1985a) has identified a number of irrational beliefs psychotherapists hold, which if left unchallenged will lead to ineffective therapy and possible therapist burnout. We suggest that you give careful consideration to these irrationalities. Take for example this unrealistic notion, "I have to be successful with all of my clients practically all of the time." Believing this, if your alcoholic client "slips" (relapses) to dysfunctional drinking, you may be prone to label yourself as a failure. Clearly, however, you will not be successful in helping every alcoholic stop and stay stopped. Slips on the road to recovery are the rule, not the exception. As such, they can often be useful experiences in the developmental process of long-term change. Damning yourself for this occurrence is therefore not only needlessly upsetting but countertherapeutic. Defending yourself from such "failure" also leads you to irrationally blame clients for their failure. This, of course, only compounds their problem. Blaming the clients may also lead to anger at them, and that can end the therapeutic relationship.

Another common irrational belief you may hold is "I must be an outstanding therapist, clearly better than other therapists I know or hear about." If you do hold this belief, the problem of therapeutic success or failure becomes even more acute. Demanding that the alcoholic client succeed so that you will be seen as an outstanding therapist by others and as having the best approach to treating alcoholics, will lead to dogmatic inflexibility – which will not help clients learn independent rational thinking. It also can make you emotionally dependent on the client and lead to depression and disillusionment. Alcoholics may be quite sensitive to this type of dependency from others and may respond to your therapy in resistant, oppositional and hostile ways. When you elevate your desire for being outstanding — "better than" — others into a dire *need to be*, you will quite likely get into therapeutic trouble.

If you have an irrational need for your clients' approval you will also court distress and emotional dependence that will be counterthera- peutic for them. If you irrationally believe "I must be greatly respected and loved by all of my clients," you are in for trouble when they often behave in a disrespectful or disapproving way. Al- though it can be argued that clients who like you are more open to your influence, some alcoholic clients will almost certainly dislike you for a whole variety of reasons. Moreover, clients who really like you may also be less willing to admit their lapses, and your relationship could interfere with good treatment. Believing your clients *must* like you may also lead you to agree with your clients' addictive thinking in order to avoid their disapproval. Although both of you may "feel" better with this approach, neither of you will benefit from this form of dependence for very long.

Another kind of self-defeating emotional indulgence stems from the erroneous belief that "Because I am a person in my own right, I must be able to enjoy myself during therapy sessions and to use these sessions to solve my personal problems as much as to help clients with their difficulties." It seems clear that therapeutic work with alcoholic clients is unlikely to be "fun" all of the time. To stay directive, use time judiciously, and persist despite clients' resistance, for therapy cannot always be enjoyable. In fact sometimes it is exhausting, difficult, and even boring. Hard work is hard work. Regardless of this fact, being productive in therapy can be enjoyable if you demand no guarantee that it will always be "a day at the beach."

Similarly, there is no evidence that therapy is a good place in which to work out your personal problems rather than help alcoholic clients work out their own. The client's welfare, not your own, is of paramount ethical and practical importance. While doing RET can certainly help you learn to think more rationally about your own life, this is an incidental rather than a primary benefit of therapy. Alcoholics and substance abusers are reluctant to come into therapy in the first place, resistant to staying with it for very long, and very unlikely to do so in order to indulge your "need" or hobby of self-improvement. Therapy is serious business for most of them. Although you would do well to spend some time and effort working on thinking rationally about yourself in relation to your client, when your thoughts and feelings about the client and your life problems become the focus of therapy, something is seriously out of line. The notion that the therapist is the main client can easily result in ineffective treatment, in dissatisfied clients, and in violations of accepted codes of professional ethics.

Another misconception held by some therapists is the belief that, "since I am doing my best and working so hard as a therapist, my clients should be equally hard working and responsible, should listen to me carefully, and should always push themselves to change." To demand this from most alcoholics and substance abusers is to practically guarantee emotional dysfunction. You then insist that clients be free of part of their major constellation of problems — namely, low frustration tolerance and rebellion — that are often the heart of their addiction. It is certainly desirable for therapists and clients to work hard, but it does not necessarily follow that a large number of clients will do so. Blaming these clients for the attitudes and habits that define their addiction is clearly countertherapeutic.

Condemning and rejecting addicts for their "lack of motivation" is a somewhat more sophisticated variety of the moralizing about alcoholism and addiction that has rarely been of much value in the past. Our job as rational-emotive therapists working with alcoholics is to motivate them — not damn them for the very problems that they have come to us for help with.

Your misconceptions and overgeneralizations about alcoholism and alcoholics can also lead to personal distress and ineffective treatment. When you believe that all alcoholics are dependent, oppositional, unmotivated, or whatever, you lead yourself into a real dead end. This kind of labeling hardly encourages emotional insight or long-term change for the client. Even if you are a recovering alcoholic or substance abuser yourself, the most that you can say objectively is that you know how your own recovery worked. It is clearly unscientific to make unsupported generalizations based on a single case, no matter how well you think you know its details. It is far better to apply the hypothesis-testing approach we advocate in RET and let the clients confirm or disconfirm your ideas about their problems. Likewise generalizations based on ethnic background, race, sex, and/or social class are misleading. It is far more rational to view your clients as persons who are alcoholic rather than as "alcholics" or "alcoholic people". Then proceed to know about and work with them on the finite set of traits, characteristics, or behaviors defining their diagnosis. You are better off letting them speak for themselves rather than demanding implicitly that they conform to your generalizations.

In most of the misconceptions we have been discussing there is a common problem, namely the therapist coming to need irrationally or depend upon the client for emotional gratification. When our sense of self, of accomplishment, or of pleasure depends on the client, we are in for trouble. Ironically, this may be an addiction in itself. Our perfectionistic demands for success, approval, enjoyment, or hard-working ideal clients are going to be frequently frustrated when we work with a number of difficult customers. Holding on to these ideas is self-defeating. They encourage the burnout most of us would prefer to avoid. They can also lead us to struggle with clients in a pointless contest over who is in charge of the therapy.

Most importantly, therapist irrationalities cloud their objectivity, distort their appreciation of the client as a person, and present dysfunctional models to the client, often resulting in less efficient and less successful treatment. Persist, therefore, in identifying your own misconceptions and work hard at giving them up or replacing them with more rational, realistic, and objective ideas about yourself and the therapeutic process.

SELF-SUPERVISION FOR OPTIMAL THERAPY

Since we have discussed in the previous section the kinds of thinking that are likely to get us into trouble as therapists and lead to personal distress as well as poor results for our clients, we will discuss the attitudes and skills we believe are most likely to lead to optimal RET with alcoholic and other substance abusing clients. Ellis (1985a) has described what he believes to be some of the characteristics of the most effective psychotherapists, rational emotive or otherwise. These characteristics, which are fully presented in Table 12.1, include 13 "ideals" or goals that the most effective therapists seem to strive toward, although they are far from perfect in achieving them.

As you will note in reviewing Table 12.1, these ideals describe psychotherapists who demonstrate a vital and enthusiastic interest in the work of helping clients change. They are knowledgeable about the various scientifically validated methods or techniques for helping the most difficult clients change and they work to apply these methods flexibly and undogmatically toward the problems of specific clients. They are effective communicators and teachers who are able to cope with their own emotional and behavioral disturbances so as not to let them interfere with their effectiveness. They are ethically responsible, professionally appropriate, and nonexploitive in their therapeutic relationships. They are encouraging, realistically optimistic, and unprejudiced toward the client, thereby unconditionally accepting clients as humans, while persistently and patiently working to help them learn to change their presenting symptoms and their self-defeating philosophies that help create these symptoms.

Difficult customers, who are likely to have a high percentage of alcoholic and substance-abusing clients among them, truly test your ability to strive for these ideals. It is relatively easy to be a good

TABLE 12.1.

Characteristics of Effective Therapists

I still take the stand I took a quarter of a century ago when I objected to Rogers' (1957) seminal papers, "The Necessary and Sufficient Conditions of Therapeutic Personality Change," and pointed out "that although basic constructive personality change — as opposed to symptom removal — seems to require fundamental modifications in the ideologies and value systems of the disturbed individual, there is probably no single condition which is absolutely necessary for the inducement of such changed attitudes and behavior patterns." (Ellis, 1959; 1962, p. 119).

With some amount of temerity, however, let me hazard the guess that when the facts have been more diligently researched, we will find that the most effective therapists tend to practice somewhat as follows:

1. They are vitally interested in helping their clients and energetically work to fulfill this interest.
2. They unconditionally accept their clients as people, while opposing and trying to ameliorate some of their self-defeating ideas, feelings, and behaviors.
3. They are confident of their own therapeutic ability and, without being rigid or grandiose, strongly believe that their main techniques will work.
4. They have a wide knowledge of therapeutic theories and practices and are flexible, undogmatic and scientific and consequently open to the acquiring of new skills and to experimenting with skills.
5. They are effective at communicating and at teaching their clients new ways of thinking, emoting, and behaving.
6. They are able to cope with and ameliorate their own disturbances and consequently are not inordinately anxious, depressed, hostile, self-downing, self-pitying or undisciplined.
7. They are patient, persistent, and hard working in their therapeutic endeavours.
8. They are ethical and responsible, and use therapy almost entirely for the benefit of clients and not for personal indulgence.
9. They act professionally and appropriately in a therapeutic setting but are still able to maintain some degree of humanness, spontaneity, and personal enjoyment in what they are doing.
10. They are encouraging and optimistic and show clients that, however difficult it may be, they can appreciably change. At times, they forcefully urge and push clients to change.
11. They not only try to help clients feel better and surrender their presenting symptoms, but also try to help them make profound attitudinal changes that will enable them to maintain their improvement, continue to improve, and ward off future disturbances.
12. They are eager to help virtually all their clients, freely refer to other therapists those they think they cannot help or are not interested in helping, and try to be neither underinvolved not overinvolved with those clients they retain. They sincerely try to overcome their strong biases for or against their clients that may interfere with their therapeutic effectiveness. They monitor their prejudices (countertransference feelings) that lead to strongly favoring or disfavoring some of their clients and, if advisable, refer such clients to other therapists.
13. They possess sufficient observational ability, sensitivity to others, good intelligence and sound judgment to discourage their clients from making rash and foolish decisions and from seriously harming themselves. (Ellis, 1985a, pp. 162–163).

therapist with willing, intelligent, cooperative, and "not too seriously disturbed" clients. The litmus test of your rationality about psychotherapy is the client who tests your acceptance of your ideal goals with repeated failures in attempts to give up self-defeating thoughts and actions. This describes exactly what often happens in working with alcoholic and substance-abusing clients. Effective therapy involves your giving unconditional acceptance by persistently and patiently working with these clients despite setbacks.

You had better avoid being authoritarian, dogmatic, or absolutistic as to how clients should or must change. It is sometimes difficult to remain active, directive, and persuasive without ignoring clients' rights to make self-defeating choices. Helping clients to take the consequences of their choices is not promoted if you are a therapist who would rather be "right" than accepting, or if your own discomfort anxiety makes you write off as unmotivated those clients who are having a hard time learning how to change.

To help with self-supervision of your attitudes toward difficult customers, we have prepared a list of admittedly rhetorical questions you can well ask yourself about such cases. These are presented in Table 12.2.

They are intended to promote self-examination and honest self-appraisal rather than perfectionism. The answers you come up with to these questions may well direct ycu toward rethinking some issues or arranging discussion with a more objective and/or experienced psychotherapist-supervisor, or in some cases asking for clarifying feedback from the clients.

In some instances, you may find it useful to discover what clients think of your persistence or flexibility. You can also objectify self-supervision — re-viewing tapes and notes on some sessions and applying the questions in Table 12.2 to obtain the advantage of distancing.

Self-supervision can be helped by your regularly reviewing the effectiveness of your work from the standpoint of therapeutic process and technique. As supervisors and trainers of rational-emotive therapists, we have found that there is occasionally a big difference between a therapist's theoretical understanding of clients' problems and the implementation of an effective plan to address their problems. Understanding clients' ABCs is fine, but it may not lead to persistently working on them session after session. Staying on target with resistant clients can be difficult. But even the best therapy plan is of little value to clients if it is not followed regularly.

You cannot easily say that RET for a given alcoholic or substance user has been ineffective unless you have used it persistently. To help

E-RET—K

TABLE 12.2.

Self-Supervision of Therapists' Approaches and Attitudes with
Alcoholic and Substance-Abusing Clients

1. Do I communicate an interest in helping my client enthusiastically and persistently even when she does not appear that interested in helping herself?

2. Am I realistically confident of my ability to help this client and do I believe in the clinical utility and scientifically demonstrated effectiveness of the methods and techniques I select to use with him?

3. Do I give individual and careful consideration to the methods and approaches I use with this client and am I willing to learn new ones and try them if the ones I select are not reasonably helpful?

4. Am I free of overt or covert stereotyped prejudice or dogmatic thinking about this client and her problem with alcohol or drugs?

5. Am I communicating effectively with this client in the vocabulary I use, my level of abstraction, cognitive style, and the way I interact with the client?

6. Do I honestly accept this client as a person — no matter how rottenly he behaves toward others and myself — while vigorously and persuasively opposing the self-defeating habits of thinking and feeling that result in such rotten behavior?

7. Do I maintain a patient, persistent and hard-working attitude toward this client despite her apparent rejection of or poor response to my efforts?

8. Am I encouraging this client's efforts while refraining from condemning her failures in order to promote the client's self-acceptance?

9. Do I overtly and covertly behave in an ethical, professional, appropriate, respectful and non-exploitive way toward this client?

10. Do I acknowledge any strong negative attitudes or feelings toward this client or about my therapeutic efforts with him and either work to eliminate them or consider the advisability of referring this client to another therapist.

self-supervise, the session-notes format used at the Institute for RET in New York is offered as Table 12.3. This form was developed for use in supervising trainees in the Institutes Fellowship program and also as part of a large outcome study of RET, which is now in progress. On it are listed the therapeutic activities and techniques that are considered integral parts of RET. Using a format like this to record each session can help you determine if what you are doing matches your perception of the clients' goals, and also if your approach is balanced and consistent over several sessions. It can also alert you to techniques or strategies you are neglecting and to the desirability for flexibility in your approach. This self-checking can also remind you to take advantage of the technical eclecticism of RET and challenge you to include new techniques that may work best for individual clients. This can also remind you that trying a given technique only once or twice is hardly a definitive test of its clinical validity.

TABLE 12.3.

Institute for RET Session Notes Form

Session :............................... .... Date..........

1. Assessing the presence of dysfunctional emotions or behaviors	( )
2. Exploring the adaptability of the client's emotions and behaviors.	( )
3. Assessing the presence and type of dysfunction cognitions.	( )
4. Exploring the adaptability of the client's belief system.	( )
5. Clarifying the activating events.	( )
6. Offering the client a hypothesis about what irrational belief the client is holding.	( )
7. Teaching the B → C connection.	( )
8. Teaching the difference between irrational and rational beliefs.	( )
9. Offering alternative rational beliefs to replace the client's irrational beliefs.	( )
10. Philosphical disputing.	( )
11. Rational-emotive imagery.	( )
12. Assigning homework.	( )
13. Assessing the client's emotions, thoughts, and behaviors that occurred when the client tried to implement a homework assignment.	( )
14. Empirical disputing.	( )
15. Instruction for rehearsal of self-statements.	( )
16. Helping the client generate alternative solutions to practical problems.	( )
17. Helping the client evaluate the effectiveness of alternative solutions.	( )
18. Behavioral rehearsal of new solutions to practical problems.	( )
19. Relaxation training or relaxing imagery.	( )

Rate the client's attempts to complete homework from the last session.

1. Made no attempt at homework.	( )
2. Made a partial attempt at homework.	( )
3. Completed some of the homework.	( )
4. Completed most of the homework.	( )
5. Completed all of the homework.	( )

Comments: ....
....
....

In addition to the information in Table 12.3, there are also some useful guidelines that apply specifically to alcoholic and substance-abusing clients. Again for purpose of self-supervision, we have developed these as a series of questions you can ask yourself about a given session with a specific client. These guidelines are presented in Table 12.4. An honest appraisal of your performance obtained through applying these questions may help redirect your work, keep you on target, or confirm that you are on the right track but had better patiently persist in what you are doing.

E-RET—L

TABLE 12.4.

Self-Supervision Guidelines for RET with Alcohol and Substance Abuse Problems

Questions that you may pose to yourself about each session:

1. Have I been active, directive, involved, and used time judiciously?
2. Have I avoided criticism of the client as a person while persuasively and persistently helping her identify and work on her problems?
3. Have I collaboratively defined the goals of the session and redirected the client's attention to these goals when indicated?
4. Have I increased the client's awareness of and curiosity about his thinking and helped his connect these thoughts to feelings?
5. Have I helped the client connect thoughts and feelings to the problem with alcohol or other substances?
6. Have I been specific and concrete in my questions to the client and my hypotheses about the connections between her thoughts, feelings, and actions?
7. Have I inquired about the client's thinking or self-talk when significant events or feelings are reported, particularly those that take place within the therapy session?
8. Have I avoided overgeneralized, all-or-nothing, and fictional interpretations of the client's problems and worked to correct them when offered by the client?
9. Have I persistently offered and specifically disputed the client's low frustration tolerance and discomfort anxiety beliefs each time they have been identified?
10. Did I review with the client the homework assigned at the last session and involve the client in a collaborative effort to design homework for this session?
11. Have I induced the client to review and monitor progress and encouraged him to share reviews with me?
12. Above all, have I been specific and convincing in my efforts to dispute the client's irrational ideas and to teach him to identify and dispute these ideas when they come up in day-to-day life?

CONCLUSIONS

No treatment of therapist survival skills for those working with alcoholics and substance-abusing clients would be complete without our strongly suggesting that you use common sense and take care of yourself as you pursue this work. Rational thinking and efforts toward self-supervision are crucial, but too much of anything is simply too much. Doing this demanding work and striving to do it effectively is likely to be quite energy consuming. Care for yourself in a reasonable and sensible way by varying your routine and avoiding overload. Anything done immoderately, even RET with alcoholics, is likely to be self-defeating. With this basic caution, let us say that doing RET can be most challenging, productive, and satisfying work. Our alcohol- and drug-abusing society can certainly benefit from its effective and efficient practice.

References

Alcoholics Anonymous. (1985). *Alcoholics Anonymous 3rd ed.* New York: Alcoholics Anonymous World Services.

American Psychiatric Association. (1980). *Diagnostic and statistical manual.* (3rd ed.) Washington, DC: American Psychiatric Association.

Bandura, A. (1977). *Social learning theory.* Englewood Cliffs, NJ: Prentice-Hall.

Bandura, A. (1982). Self-efficacy mechanism in human agency. *American Psychologist.* 97(2), 122–147.

Bard, J. (1980). *Rational-emotive therapy in practice.* Champaign, IL: Research Press.

Beck, A. T. (1976). *Cognitive therapy and the emotional disorders.* New York: International Universities Press.

Beck, A. T., Rush, A. J., Shaw, B. F., & Emery, G. (1979). *Cognitive therapy of depression.* New York: Guilford Press.

Bellack, A. S., & Hersen, M. (Eds.). (1985). *Dictionary of behavior therapy techniques.* New York: Pergamon.

Bernard, M. E. (1986). *Staying alive in an irrational world: The philosophy of Albert Ellis.* Melbourne: Macmillan.

Bernard, M., & DiGiuseppe, R. (in press). *Inside RET: A critical appraisal of the theory and therapy of Albert Ellis.* Orlando, FL: Academic Press.

Bohman, M. (1978). Some genetic aspects of alcoholism and criminality. *Archives of General Psychiatry, 35,* 269–276.

Bone, H. (1968). Two proposed alternatives to psychoanalytic interpreting. In E. Hammer (Ed.), *Use of interpretation in treatment* (pp. 169–196). New York: Grune & Stratton.

Brandsma, J. M. (1980). *Outpatient treatment of alcoholism: A review and comparative study.* Baltimore, MD: University Park Press.

Brown, S. (1985). *Treating the alcoholic: A developmental model of recovery.* New York: Wiley.

Brownell, K. D., Marlatt, G. A., Lichtenstein, E., & Wilson, G. T. (1986). Understanding and preventing relapses. *American Psychologist, 41,* 765–782.

Calahan, D., & Room, R. (1972). Problem drinking among American men aged 21–59. *American Journal of Public Health, 62,* 1473–1482.

Carey, K. B., & Maisto, S. A. (1985). A review of the use of self-control techniques in the treatment of alcohol abuse. *Cognitive Therapy and Research, 9,* 235–251.

Cleckley, H. (1982). *The mask of sanity.* St. Louis: Mosby.

Corey, G. (1985). *Theory and practice of group counseling.* (2nd ed.). Monterey, CA: Brooks/Cole.

Corey, G. (1986). *Theory and practice of counselling and psychotherapy.* (3rd ed.) Monterey, CA: Brooks/Cole.

Craighead, E. C., Kazdin, A. E., & Mahoney, M. (1981). *Behavior modification: Principles, issues and applications (2nd edition).* Boston: Houghton Mifflin.

149

Critchlow, B. (1986). The powers of John Barleycorn: Beliefs about the effects of alcohol on social behaviours. *American Psychologist, 41*, 751–764.

DiGiuseppe, R. (1983). RET with conduct disorder. In A. Ellis & M. Bernard (Eds.), *Rational emotive approach to the problems of childhood*. New York: Plenum.

DiGiuseppe, R. (1986). The implications of the philosophy of science for rational-emotive theory and therapy. *Psychotherapy, 23*, 634–639.

DiGiuseppe, R. (in press). Cognitive behavior therapy with families of conduct disorder in children. In N. Epstein, S. Schebinger, & W. Dryden (Eds.), *Cognitive behavior therapy with families*. New York: Brunner/Mazel.

Dryden, W. (1984). *Rational-emotive therapy: Fundamentals and innovations*. Beckenham, Kent: Croom-Helm.

Dryden, W., & Trower, P. (Eds.). (1986). *Rational-emotive therapy: Recent developments in theory and practice*. Bristol, England: Institute for RET (UK).

Ellis, A. (1956). The effectiveness of psychotherapy with individuals who have severe homosexual problems. *Journal of Counselling Psychology, 20*, 191–195.

Ellis, A. (1957a). *How to live with a neurotic: At home and at work*. New York: Crown. (Revised ed., Hollywood, CA, Wilshire, 1975.)

Ellis, A. (1957b). Outcome of employing three techniques of psychotherapy. *Journal of Clinical Psychology, 13*, 344–350.

Ellis, A. (1958a). Rational psychotherapy. *Journal of General Psychology, 59*, 35–49. (Reprinted, New York, Institute for Rational-Emotive Therapy.)

Ellis, A. (1958b). *Sex without guilt*. New York: Lyle Stuart. (Revised ed, Secaucus, NJ: Lyle Stuart, 1965.)

Ellis, A. (1959). Requisite conditions for basic personality change. *Journal of Consulting Psychology, 23*, 538–540.

Ellis, A. (1962). *Reason and emotion in psychotherapy*. Secaucus, NJ: Citadel Press.

Ellis, A. (1963a). *Sex and the single man*. Secaucus, NJ: Lyle Stuart.

Ellis, A. (1963b). *The intelligent woman's guide to manhunting*. Secaucus, NJ: Lyle Stuart.

Ellis, A. (1968). *Homework report*. New York: Institute for Rational-Emotive Therapy.

Ellis, A. (1969a). A weekend of rational encounter. *Rational Living, 4*(2), 1–8.

Ellis, A. (1969b). A cognitive approach to behavior therapy. *International Journal of Psychiatry, 8*, 896–900.

Ellis, A. (1971). *Growth through reason*. North Hollywood, CA: Wilshire.

Ellis, A. (1972a). *Psychotherapy and the value of a human being*. New York: Institute for Rational-Emotive Therapy.

Ellis, A. (1972b). *Conquering low frustration tolerance* (Cassette recording). New York: Institute for Rational-Emotive Therapy.

Ellis, A. (1973a). *Humanistic psychotherapy: The rational-emotive approach*. New York: McGraw-Hill.

Ellis, A. (1973b). *Twenty-one ways to stop worrying* (Cassette recording). New York: Institute for Rational-Emotive Therapy.

Ellis, A. (1973c). *How to stubbornly refuse to be ashamed of anything* (Cassette recording). New York: Institute for Rational-Emotive Therapy.

Ellis, A. (1976a). *Sex and the liberated man*. Secaucus, NJ: Lyle Stuart.

Ellis, A. (1976b). The biological basis of human irrationality. *Journal of Individual Psychology, 32*, 145–168. (Reprinted) New York, Institute for Rational-Emotive Therapy.,

Ellis, A. (1976c). RET abolishes most of the human ego. *Psychotherapy, 13*, 343–348. (Reprinted, New York, Institute for Rational-Emotive Therapy.)

Ellis, A. (1977a). Fun as psychotherapy. *Rational Living, 12*(1), 2–6.

Ellis, A. (Speaker). (1977b). *A garland of rational humorous songs* (Cassette recording). New York: Institute for Rational-Emotive Therapy.

Ellis, A. (1978). *I'd like to stop but . . . Dealing with addictions* (Cassette recording). New York: Institute for Rational-Emotive Therapy.

Ellis, A. (1978–1979). Discomfort anxiety: A new cognitive behavioral construct. Parts I and II. *Rational Living, 14*(2), 3–8; *15*(1), 25–30.

Ellis, A. (1979a). Rejoinder: Elegant and inelegant RET. In A. Ellis & J. M. Whiteley (Eds.), *Theoretical and empirical foundation of rational-emotive therapy* (pp. 240–267). Monterey, CA: Brooks/Cole.

Ellis, A. (1979b). *The intelligent woman's guide to dating and mating.* Secaucus, NJ: Lyle Stuart.

Ellis, A. (1979c). Rational-emotive therapy: Research data that support the clinical and personality hypotheses of RET and other modes of cognitive-behavior therapy. In A. Ellis & J. M. Whiteley (Eds.), *Theoretical and empirical foundations of rational-emotive therapy* (pp. 101–173). Monterey, CA: Brooks/Cole.

Ellis, A. (1980). Rational-emotive therapy and cognitive behavior therapy: Similarities and differences. *Cognitive Therapy and Research, 4,* 325–340.

Ellis, A. (1981, October 4). *Case presentations: The Ellis approach to specific kinds of clients in therapy.* Workshop presented in Charlotte, NC.

Ellis, A. (1982a). The treatment of alcohol and drug abuse: A rational-emotive approach. *Rational Living, 17*(2), 15–24.

Ellis, A. (1982b, November 3). *Workshop in rational-emotive therapy and alcohol and drug abuse.* Institute for Integral Development, Colorado Springs.

Ellis, A. (1984). The essence of RET – 1984. *Journal of Rational-Emotive Therapy, 2*(1), 19–25.

Ellis, A. (1985a). *Overcoming resistance: Rational-emotive therapy with difficult clients.* New York: Springer.

Ellis, A. (1985b). Expanding the ABCs of rational-emotive therapy. In M. Mahoney & A. Freeman (Eds.), *Cognition and psychotherapy* (pp. 313–323). New York: Plenum.

Ellis, A. (1986). An emotional control card for inappropriate and appropriate emotions in using rational-emotive imagery. *Journal of Counseling and Devleopment, 65,* 205–206.

Ellis, A. (1987). The use of rational humorous songs in psychotherapy. In W. F, Fry, Jr. & W. A., Salameh (Eds.), *Handbook of humor and psychotherapy* (pp. 265–287). Sarasota, FL: Professional Resource Exchange.

Ellis, A., & Abrahms, E. (1978). *Brief psychotherapy in medical and health practice.* New York: Springer.

Ellis, A., & Becker, I. (1982). *A guide to personal happiness.* North Hollywood, CA: Wilshire.

Ellis, A., & Bernard, M. E. (Eds.). (1984). *Rational-emotive approaches to the problems of childhood.* New York: Plenum.

Ellis, A., & Bernard, M. E. (Eds.). (1985b). *Clinical applications of rational-emotive therapy.* New York: Plenum.

Ellis, A., & Dryden, W. (1987). *The practice of rational-emotive therapy.* New York: Springer.

Ellis, A., & Grieger, R. (Eds.). (1986). *Handbook of rational-emotive therapy* (2 vols.). New York: Springer.

Ellis, A., & Harper, R. A. (1975). *A new guide to rational living.* North Hollywood, CA: Wilshire.

Ellis, A., & Grieger, R. (Eds.). (1977). Handbook of rational-emotive therapy (vol. 1). New York: Springer.

Ellis, A., & Harper, R. A. (1961). *A guide to a successful marriage.* North Hollywood, CA: Wilshire.

Ellis, A., & Knaus, W. (1977). *Overcoming procrastination.* New York: New American Library.

Ellis, A., & Whiteley, J. M. (Eds.). (1979). *Theoretical and empirical foundations of rational-emotive therapy.* Monterey, CA: Brooks/Cole.

Franks, L. (1985, October 20). A new attack on alcoholism. *The New York Times Magazine.* pp. 47–67.

Freeman, A. (1987). Cognitive therapy: An overview. In A. Freeman, & V. Greenwood (Eds.). *Cognitive therapy: Application in psychiatric and medical setting* (pp. 19–35). New York: Human Sciences Press.

Glueck, S., & Glueck, E. (1950). *Unravelling juvenile delinquency.* New York: The Commonwealth Fund.

Goodwin, D. W. (1976). *Is alcoholism hereditary?* New York: Oxford University Press.

Goodwin, D. W. (1979). Alcoholism and heredity. *Archives of General Psychiatry, 36,* 57–61.

Goodwin, D. W., Schulsinger, F., Hermansen, L., Guze, S. B., & Winokur, G. (1973). Alcohol problems in adoptees raised apart from biological parents. *Archives of General Psychiatry, 28,* 238–243.

Gorman, J. N., & Rooney, J. S. (1979). The influence of Al-Anon on the coping behavior of wives and alcoholics. *Journal of Studies on Alcohol, 40,* 1030–1038.

Greenwood, V. (1985). RET and substance abuse. In A. Ellis & M. Bernard (Eds.), *Clinical applications of RET* (pp. 209–235). New York: Plenum.

Grieger, R., & Boyd, J. (1980). *Rational-emotive therapy: A skills-based approach.* New York: Van Nostrand Reinhold.

Grieger, R., & Grieger, I. (Eds.). (1982). *Cognition and emotional disturbance.* New York: Human Sciences Press.

Gutsch, K. U., Sisemore, D. A., & Williams, R. L. (1984). *Systems of psychotherapy.* Springfield, IL: C. Thomas.

Hare, R. D. (1986). Twenty years of experience with the Cleckley psychopath. In W. H. Reid, D. Dorr, J. I. Walker, & J. W. Bonner, III (Eds.), *Unmasking the psychopath: Antisocial personality and related syndrome.* New York: Norton.

Heesacker, M., Heppner, P. P., & Rogers, M. E. (1982). Classics and emerging classics in psychology. *Journal of Counseling Psychology, 29,* 400–405.

Jacobsen, E. (1938). *You must relax.* New York: McGraw-Hill.

Jellinek, E. M. (1960). *The disease concept of alcoholism.* New Haven: Hillhouse Press.

Kurtz, E. (1979). *Not-God: A history of alcoholics anonymous.* Center City, MN: Hazelden Educational Services.

Lazarus, A. A. (1977). Toward an egoless state of being. In A. Ellis & R. Grieger (Eds.). *Handbook of rational-emotive therapy.* Vol. 1 (pp. 113–116). New York: Springer.

Lazarus, R. S. (1966). *Psychological stress and the coping process.* New York: McGraw-Hill.

Levison, P. K., Gerstein, D. R., & Maloff, D. R. (Eds.). (1983). *Commonalities in substance abuse and habitual behavior.* Lexington, MA: Lexington.

Marlatt, G. A., (1983). The controlled drinking controversy: A commentary. *American Psychologist, (10),* 1097–1110.

Marlatt, G. A. & Gordon, J. R. (1985). *Relapse prevention: Maintenance strategies in the treatment of addictive behaviors.* New York. Guilford.

Maultsby, M. C., Jr. (1975). *Help yourself to happiness: Through rational self-counseling.* New York: Institute for Rational-Emotive Therapy.

Maultsby, M. C., Jr. (1978). *A million dollars for your hangover.* Lexington, KY: Rational Self-Help Books.

Maultsby, M. C., Jr. (1979). *Freedom from alcohol and tranquilizers.* Lexington, KY. Rational Self-Help Aids.

Maultsby, M. C., Jr., & Ellis, A. (1974). *Technique for using rational-emotive imagery.* New York: Institute for Rational-Emotive Therapy.

McClearn, C. (1981). Genetic studies in animals. *Alcoholism: Clinical and Experimental Research, 5,* 447–448.

McCord, W., & McCord. J. (1960). *Origins of Alcoholism*, Stanford, CA: Stanford University Press.

Meichenbaum, D. (1977). *Cognitive-behavior modification*. New York: Plenum.

Miller, T. (1983). *So you secretly suspect you're worthless, well . . .* Manilus, NY: Author.

Miller, W. R. (1976). Alcoholism scales and objective assessment methods: A review. *Psychological Bulletin, 83,* 649–674.

Miller, W. R. (1983). Controlled drinking: A history and critical review. *Journal of Studies on Alcohol, 44,* 68–83.

Miller, W. R. (1985). Motivation for treatment: A review with special emphasis on alcoholism. *Psychological Bulletin, 98*(1), 84–107.

Miller, W. R., & Hester, R. K. (1980). Treating the problem drinker: Modern approaches. In W. R. Miller (Ed.), *The addictive behaviors: Treatment of alcoholism, drug abuse, smoking, and obesity* (pp. 11–141). Oxford, England: Pergamon.

Moreno, J. L. (1966, April). Therapeutic aspects of psychodrama. *Psychiatric Opinion*, pp. 36–42.

Nathan, P. E. (1980). Etiology and process in the addictive behaviors. In W. R. Miller (Ed.), *The addictive behaviors: Treatment of alcoholism, drug abuse, smoking and obesity* (pp. 241–264). Oxford, England: Pergamon.

Nathan, P. E., Titler, N. A., Lowenstein, L. M., Solomon, P., & Rossi, A. M. (1970). Behavioral analysis of chronic alcoholism. *Archives of General Psychiatry, 22,* 419–430.

National Institute on Drug Abuse. (1979). *Behavioral analysis and treatment of substance abuse* (NIDA Research Monograph No. 25), Washington, DC: U.S. Department of Health Education and Welfare.

Orford, J. (1985). *Excessive appetites: A psychological view of addictions.* New York: Wiley.

Paolino, T. J., & McGrady, B. S. (1977). *The alcoholic marriage.* New York: Grune & Stratton.

Quayle, D. (1983). American productivity: the devastating effect of alcoholism and drug abuse. *American Psychologist, 38*(4), 454–458.

Robins, L. N. (1966). *Deviant children grown up: A sociological and psychiatric study of sociopathic personality.* Baltimore: Williams & Wilkins.

Rogers, C. R. (1957). The necessary and sufficient conditions of therapeutic personality change. *Journal of consulting psychology, 21,* 859–861.

Rogers, C. R. (1961). *On becoming a person.* Boston: Houghton-Mifflin.

Royce, J. E. (1981). *Alcohol problems and alcoholism.* New York: Free Press.

Rutstein, D. D., & Veech, R. (1978). Genetics and addiction to alcohol. *New England Journal of Medicine, 298,* 1140–1141.

Schuckitt, M. (1973). Alcoholism and sociopathy — diagnostic confusion. *Quarterly Journal of Studies in Alcohol, 34,* 157–164.

Schuckitt, M. A. (1981). The genetics of alcoholism. *Alcoholism: Clinicial and Experimental Research, 5,* 439–440.

Seligman, M. E. P. (1975). *Helplessness.* San Francisco: Freeman.

Seizer, M. L. (1971). The Michigan Alcoholism Screening Test: The quest for a new diagnostic instrument. *American Journal of Psychiatry, 127,* 1653–1658.

Sichel, J., & Ellis, A. (1984). *RET self-help form.* New York: Institute for Rational-Emotive Therapy.

Smith, D. (1982). Trends in counseling and psychotherapy. *American Psychologist, 37,* 802–809.

Vaillant, G. E. (1980). Natural custom of male psychological health, VIII: Antecedent of alcoholism and "orality". *American Journal of Psychiatry, 137,* 181–186.

Vaillant, G. E. (1983). *The natural history of alcoholism: Causes, patterns, and paths to recovery.* Cambridge, MA: Harvard University Press.

Vaillant, G. E., & Milosfsky, E. S. (1982). The etiology of Alcoholism: A prospective study. *American Psychologist, 37,* 494–503.

Velten, E. (1986). Withdrawal from heroin and methidone with Rational Emotive Therapy: theory and practice. W. Dryden & P. T. Trower (Eds.). *Rational-Emotive Therapy: Recent developments in theory and practice.* Bristol, England: Institute for Rational Emotive Therapy, United Kingdom.

Vogler, R. E. & Bartz, W. R. (1982). *The better way to drink: Moderation and control of problem drinking.* New York: Simon & Schuster.

Walen, S. R., DiGiuseppe, R., & Wessler, R. L. (1980). *A practitioner's guide to rational-emotive therapy.* New York: Oxford University Press.

Ward, R. F., & Faillace, L. A. (1970). The alcoholic and his helpers: A systems view. *Quarterly Journal of Studies on Alcohol, 31,* 684–691.

Weinrach, S. G. (1980), Unconventional therapist: Albert Ellis. *Personnel and Guidance Journal, 59,* 152–160.

Wessler, R. A., & Wessler, R. L. (1980). *The principles and practice of rational-emotive therapy.* San Francisco, CA: Jossey-Bass.

West, L. J. (1984). Alcoholism and related problems: An overview. L. J. West (Ed.), *Alcoholism and Related Problems: Issues for the American public* (pp. 1–26). Englewood Cliffs, NJ: Prentice–Hall.

Williamson, D. A. (1985). Response prevention. !n A. S. Bellack & M. Hersen (Eds.), *Dictionary of behavior therapy techniques* (pp. 185–196). New York: Pergamon.

Wolpe, J. (1982). *The practice of behavior therapy* (3rd ed.). New York: Pergamon.

Zucker, R. A., & Gomberg, E. S. L. (1986). Etiology of alcoholism reconsidered: The case for a biopsychosocial process. *American Psychologist, 41,* 783–793.

Author Index

155

Subject Index

About the Authors

Albert Ellis, Ph.D., is the founder of RET, Executive Director of the Institute for Rational-Emotive Therapy, New York City, and the author of over 50 books and 600 journal articles.

John F. McInerney, Ph.D., is an Associate Fellow and supervisor of the Institute of Rational-Emotive Therapy and in private practice in Cape May County, New Jersey.

Raymond DiGiuseppe, Ph.D., is Director of Training and Research of the Institute for Rational-Emotive Therapy in New York City; Associate Professor of Psychology, St. John's University, and co-author of *The Practitioner's Guide to RET* and *Inside RET: A critical appraisal of Albert Ellis' theory and therapy.*

Raymond J. Yeager, Ph.D., is a graduate fellow and staff therapist at the Institute of Rational-Emotive Therapy, The Director of Psychological Services at APPLE, Inc.: A Program Planned for Life Enrichment, in Hauppauge, New York, and is in private practice in Commack, New York.

Psychology Practitioner Guidebooks

Editors
Arnold P. Goldstein, Syracuse University
Leonard Krasner, Stanford University & SUNY at Stony Brook
Sol L. Garfield, Washington University

Elsie M. Pinkston & Nathan L. Linsk – CARE OF THE ELDERLY: A Family Approach

Donald Meichenbaum – STRESS INOCULATION TRAINING
Sebastiano Santostefano – COGNITIVE CONTROL THERAPY WITH CHILDREN AND ADOLESCENTS

Lillie Weiss, Melanie Katzman & Sharlene Wolchik – TREATING BULIMIA: A Psychoeducational Approach

Edward B. Blanchard & Frank Andrasik – MANAGEMENT OF CHRONIC HEADACHES: A Psychological Approach

Raymond G. Romanczyk – CLINICAL UTILIZATION OF MICROCOMPUTER TECHNOLOGY

Philip H. Bornstein & Marcy T. Bornstein – MARITAL THERAPY: A Behavioral-Communications Approach

Michael T. Nietzel & Ronald C. Dillehay – PSYCHOLOGICAL CON-SULTATION IN THE COURTROOM

Elizabeth B. Yost, Larry E. Beutler, M. Anne Corbishley & James R. Allender – GROUP COGNITIVE THERAPY: A Treatment Method for Depressed Older Adults

Lillie Weiss – DREAM ANALYSIS IN PSYCHOTHERAPY

Edward A. Kirby & Liam K. Grimley – UNDERSTANDING AND TREATING ATTENTION DEFICIT DISORDER

Jon Eisenson – LANGUAGE AND SPEECH DISORDERS IN CHIL-DREN

Eva L. Feindler & Randolph B. Ecton– ADOLESCENT ANGER CON-TROL: Cognitive-Behavioral Techniques

Michael C. Roberts – PEDIATRIC PSYCHOLOGY: Psychological Interventions and Strategies for Pediatric Problems

Daniel S. Kirschenbaum, William G. Johnson & Peter M. Stalonas, Jr. – TREATING CHILDHOOD AND ADOLESCENT OBESITY

W. Stewart Agras – EATING DISORDERS: Management of Obesity, Bulimia and Anorexia Nervosa

Ian H. Gotlib & Catherine A. Colby – TREATMENT OF DEPRESSION: An Interpersonal Systems Approach

Walter B. Pryzwansky & Robert N. Wendt – PSYCHOLOGY AS A PROFESSION: Foundations of Practice

Cynthia D. Belar, William W. Deardorff & Karen E. Kelly – THE PRACTICE OF CLINICAL HEALTH PSYCHOLOGY

Paul Karoly & Mark P. Jensen – MULTIMETHOD ASSESSMENT OF CHRONIC PAIN

William L. Golden, E. Thomas Dowd & Fred Friedberg – HYPNO-THERAPY: A Modern Approach

Patricia Lacks – BEHAVIORAL TREATMENT FOR PERSISTENT INSOMNIA

Arnold P. Goldstein & Harold Keller – AGGRESSIVE BEHAVIOR: Assessment and Intervention

C. Eugene Walker, Barbara L. Bonner & Keith L. Kaufman – THE PHYSICALLY AND SEXUALLY ABUSED CHILD: Evaluation and Treatment

Robert E. Becker, Richard G. Heimberg & Alan S. Bellack – SOCIAL SKILLS TRAINING TREATMENT FOR DEPRESSION

Richard F. Dangel & Richard A. Polster – TEACHING CHILD MAN-AGEMENT SKILLS